HANDMADE
Baby Gifts

HANDMADE
Baby Gifts

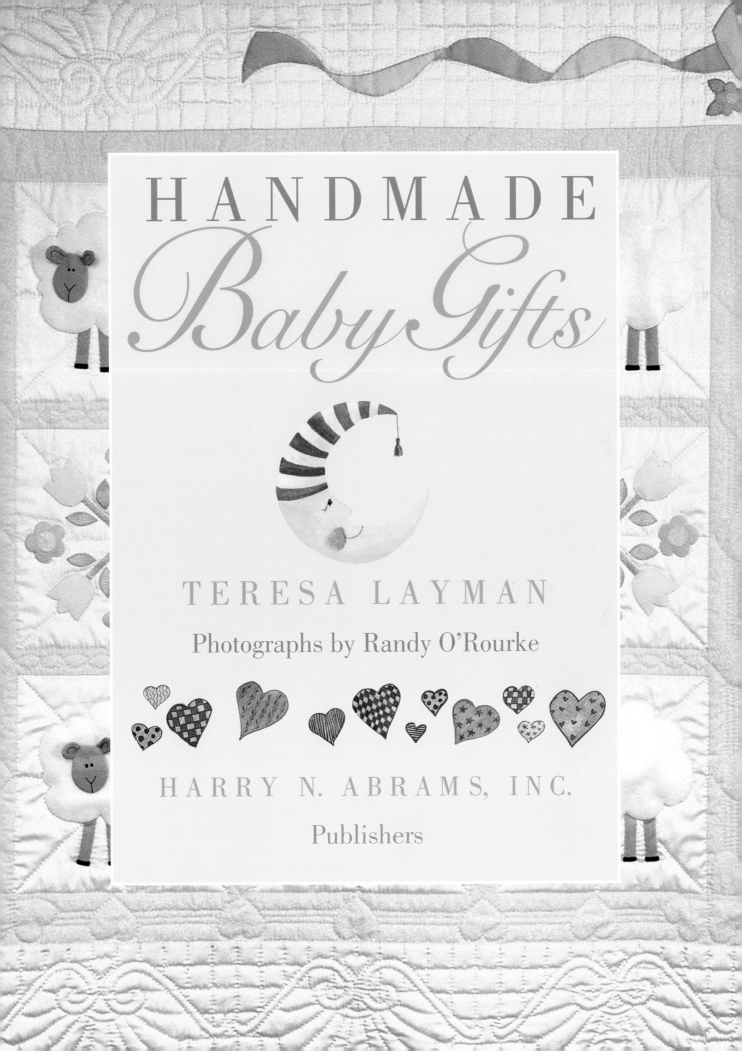

TERESA LAYMAN

Photographs by Randy O'Rourke

HARRY N. ABRAMS, INC.

Publishers

For Karen

Acknowledgments

This book came to be with the help of a large crowd of people, all of whom are appreciated in the extreme. I would like to thank the wonderful people who helped with the construction of the projects: Gretchen Mastrogiannis, Amy Stultz and Alberta Hooper, my sisters in our love of sewing and all around good friends. The production of the book was in the very capable hands of my editor, Ellen Cohen, and book designer, Judith Michael. The adorable faces in these pages belong to Emma Bushnell, William Cohen, Channél Generette, Kevin Massey, Peter Schneider, Tyler Vincent, McKenna Yanik, and Paige Yanik. Thank you to these sweet babies and their parents who allowed us to photograph them. Randy O'Rourke, photographer extraordinaire, for the hours of patience it takes to produce so many wonderful photographs. Bobbi Chase for letting us use her beautiful monogram alphabet. Ellen Prindle for letting us take over her house for a day. Cathy Yanik, Richard Palan, and Pat Calise, my friends who are always there to help me in any way. My husband, Kenny, because he's wonderful, and my daughter Karen who was the original inspiration for this book. Thank you. —T. L.

Editor: Ellen Rosefsky Cohen
Designer: Judith Michael

Library of Congress Cataloging-in-Publication Data

Layman, Teresa.
Handmade baby gifts / by Teresa Layman ; photographs by Randy O'Rourke.
p. cm.
ISBN 0–8109–4151–1
1. Sewing. 2. Needlework. 3. Infants' supplies. I. Title.   TT751.L384   1999
746—dc21   99–11061

Printed and bound in China

Harry N. Abrams, Inc.
100 Fifth Avenue
New York, N.Y. 10011
www.abramsbooks.com

Contents

Preface

When I see a beautiful baby gift that was handmade, to celebrate either a baby's birth or a christening, I know the maker wanted to keep the memory of the happy time forever. The birth of my own daughter made me feel this way, too. I wanted to cherish this wonderful time in my life and I wanted my baby to know how much she was welcomed and loved.

Since my passion lies in the needle arts, that's where I began. A birth sampler, a christening gown with her name embroidered on it, special soft clothes and blankets—all were handmade with love. By putting needle to cloth, I had created heirlooms to last a lifetime and more.

I have chosen for this book the best of the ideas and projects to share with other new mothers, grandmothers, relatives, and friends. Some of the projects here are meant to be used and loved, while others are meant to be handed down from generation to generation. There are projects that are great for beginners—even kids—who can make the baby cap, sock bunny, or washcloths. And there are projects for those who want a bit more of a challenge, like the quilt or the christening gown. There are hand-sewn, embroidered things and machine-sewn creations. Whatever your preference, if there is a baby in your future, you can find a beautiful gift to make for him or her in these pages.

Each project has a list of materials needed to create the project. In addition to those materials there are some basic sewing tools you will need:

1. Sewing machine with a zigzag stitch capability in good working order
2. New, sharp needles for your sewing machine: sizes 65/9, 70/10, and 80/12, are good choices to keep on hand
3. Pair of sharp sewing scissors that you use only for cutting fabric (cutting anything else with your good scissors will dull the blades and make fabric cutting frustrating)
4. Hand-sewing needles (my favorites are sizes 8 and 10 crewel)
5. Iron and ironing board
6. Fine shaft (0.5 mm) glass head pins
7. Tape measure
8. Good light
9. Seam ripper, just in case
10. ½″ bias tape maker (used often in these projects)
11. Rotary cutter, cutting mat, and cutting ruler are very helpful for the quilt and crib bumper projects
12. Some people find a thimble and needle-threader helpful as well

So, I invite you to choose a project or two to make for that special baby in your life, for when you give a gift that is handmade, the receiver knows it came from your heart and the gift is that much more treasured.

T. L.

Baby's Room

Cozy Blankets

MATERIALS

❧ 2 coordinating flannels (1¼ yards by 45″ each)
❧ scrap fabrics for appliqués
❧ thread to match
❧ embroidery floss (colors given with each design)

INSTRUCTIONS

Note: Patterns are on page 91. Blanket fabric is the side to be appliquéd; lining is the other side.

1. Trim both blanket fabric and lining fabric pieces to 42″ square.
2. Trace corner template onto paper.
3. Lay out fabric pieces on a flat surface, right sides together. Transfer the corner shape to the fabric corners and trim to shape. (Fig. 1)
4. Transfer desired appliqué design to one corner of the right side of the blanket fabric.
5. Transfer markings for each appliqué piece to the wrong side of the appliqué fabric. With right sides together, layer the appliqué piece and lightweight lining (this can be the same fabric if you are using a cotton broadcloth). Using a tiny stitch length, stitch around each piece. (Fig. 2)
6. Cut out each piece about ⅛″ from the stitching line. Clip corners and curves.
7. Carefully cut a slash into the lining layer of each section (Fig. 3) and turn right side out. Press. Where pattern pieces indicate, leave an opening in the seam to turn the piece right side out, as the opening will be covered by another piece.
8. Lay each piece on its place on the blanket according to the appliqué design and blindstitch in place. (Fig. 4) For the bear, add a tiny piece

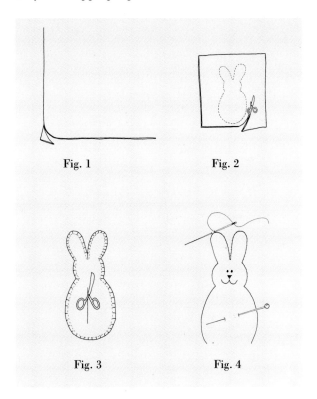

Fig. 1   Fig. 2

Fig. 3   Fig. 4

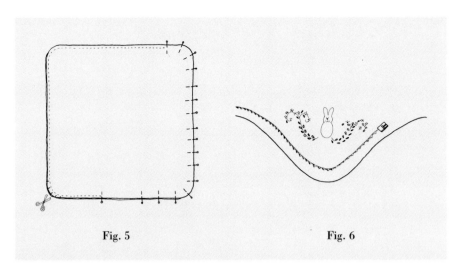

Fig. 5   Fig. 6

of lace at his neck before stitching his head in place. For the bear's juggling balls, run a hand-gathering stitch around each ball piece. Pull up gathers very tightly, adding a small piece of stuffing to each one before closing. Stitch onto the blanket smooth-side up using a blind stitch.

9. Work the embroidery design using two strands of floss according to the design diagrams.

10. Pin the blanket and lining fabrics right sides together at the raw edges. Using a ¼″ seam, stitch around the edges leaving a 6″ opening on one side for turning. Clip curves and turn right side out. (Fig. 5)

11. Turn in the seam allowance on the open edges. Slip stitch the pressed edges together.

12. Use a decorative machine stitch or hand featherstitch and stitch around the blanket 1″ in from edge. (Fig. 6)

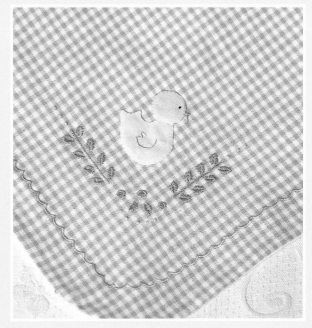

"Flowers for Ewe" Quilt

When making a quilt, first wash all the fabrics to preshrink them and to expel any extra dyes in the fabric. It will also make your fabrics softer and nicer to work with. I try to use natural fiber fabrics and battings because they stand up better to the test of time, especially if you plan on using your quilt. However, every once in a while, I find a synthetic fiber fabric that is perfect for the job at hand, as was the case with the lambs in this quilt. In general, if you choose good quality materials when you are investing your time, energy, and money in a project, your creation will look better and last longer.

When cutting and sewing the quilt pieces, *be precise*. I cannot stress this enough. Each piece in your quilt is dependent on the other pieces, and if the measurement of one piece is changed, even slightly, it will affect the rest of the quilt—especially in ease of assembly. Precision in cutting and sewing is essential to making your project a success and a pleasure to sew.

This quilt was made using a technique called machine appliqué. The appliqué pieces are first fused in place using a paper-backed fusible web. Once the pressing is complete, use a machine satin stitch to finish the raw edges of each piece. A machine satin stitch is actually just a very tight zigzag stitch. On my sewing machine the stitch width is 1½ and the length is about ¼. Try out different stitches on fabric scraps to see what you like best. Write down your favorite setting so you can easily go back to it next time. Satin stitch all the raw edges of each piece in a matching or coordinating thread color. Begin and end each line of satin stitching by locking the thread in place with a straight stitch set at zero or the shortest possible setting.

MATERIALS

- ✤ 1½ yards background fabric (ivory)
- ✤ ¾ yard sashing and border fabric (pale pink)
- ✤ ¼ yard light gray (faces and legs)
- ✤ ¼ yard fuzzy white fabric (lambs)
- ✤ ¼ yard pale green (leaves and stems)
- ✤ ¼ yard light pink (tulips and corner rose)
- ✤ ¼ yard light blue (ribbons)
- ✤ ¼ yard medium blue (ribbons and blue flowers)
- ✤ scrap of pale yellow (flower centers)
- ✤ 1 yard paper-backed fusible web
- ✤ wash-out fabric marking pen or pencil
- ✤ black fine-point permanent fabric marking pen
- ✤ thread to match fabric colors
- ✤ dark gray thread (lambs' hooves)
- ✤ quilting thread
- ✤ ½" bias tape maker (optional)
- ✤ 45" by 60" batting
- ✤ 3 yards fabric for back of quilt (or 1⅜ yard of 54" or wider fabric)
- ✤ rotary cutter, cutting board, and ruler are very helpful, but not essential

INSTRUCTIONS

Note: Patterns are on pages 92–95. All seam allowances are ¼″ unless otherwise specified. The letters in parentheses indicate pieces as labeled on the assembly diagram. The colors are included in parentheses so you can see the relationship of the colors to each other in the photograph and to clarify where each piece will go. You may wish to substitute other colors.

1. Wash, dry, and press all fabrics before cutting.
2. (A) Cut 9 squares, 9½″ by 9½″ (ivory).
   (B) Cut 6 sashing strips 1½″ by 9½″ (pale pink).
   (C) Cut 2 sashing strips 1½″ by 29½″ (pale pink).
   (D) Cut 2 sashing strips 2½″ by 29½″ (pale pink).
   (E) Cut 2 sashing strips 2½″ by 33½″ (pale pink).
   (F) Cut 4 border strips 6½″ by 33½″ (ivory).
   (G) Cut 20 corner block squares 2½″ by 2½″ (ivory).
   (H) Cut 16 corner block squares 2½″ by 2½″ (pale pink).

Lamb Blocks

1. Using wash-out marking pen or pencil, transfer the lamb design to five of the 9½″ square (A) blocks.
2. To make the lambs' legs, cut a 1″ bias strip of gray fabric 50″ long (a rotary cutter and board are the most efficient and precise way to cut these) and fold each long edge to the center and press—or run the bias strip through a ½″ bias tape maker and press. Cut the bias strip into twenty 2½″ pieces. Place four 2½″ lengths of bias tape as legs on each lamb block having one raw edge so it will be tucked under the lamb's body fabric. Stitch in place by hand or machine. Then, use a machine satin stitch set at the widest width and dark gray thread to cover the raw ends of the bias to make the lambs' hooves.
3. Trace the lamb's body onto a sheet of plain white paper, cut it out, then trace five lamb bodies in reverse onto the paper side of the fusible web. Following manufacturer's directions for heat and time, fuse the web to the wrong side of the fuzzy white lamb fabric. Cut out each one on the traced lines, then peel off the paper backing. Place each body on a lamb block, covering the top raw edges of the legs. Fuse in place (you may have to fuse it from the back side). Use a machine satin stitch to cover all raw edges of the lambs' bodies.
4. To make the lambs' faces, trace the outline of the face onto the wrong side of the gray cotton fabric. Place this piece, right sides together, with another piece of gray fabric and stitch on the traced line. (Fig. 1) Cut around the stitching lines, leaving a ⅛″ seam allowance. Clip into the corners and around the curves (Fig. 2) and carefully make a 1″ slash in the back layer. Turn right side out through the slash. Make sure the seams are turned out very crisply, you can push them out gently but firmly with a chopstick, or other such tool, and press. Draw on the faces according to the pattern using a fine-point permanent marking pen. Place and pin the lamb's head on the body as indicated on the pattern and blind stitch in place, leaving the ears free.

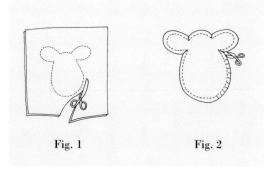

Fig. 1   Fig. 2

14

Flower Blocks

1. Using wash-out marking pen or pencil, transfer the flower design to the remaining four 9½″ square (A) blocks. Make the stems first by cutting 44″ of 1″ bias strips. Fold the long raw edges to the center and press or run it through a ½″ bias tape maker and press. Fold in half lengthwise again to make a ¼″ wide strip and press. Cut eight 5″ pieces. Place one 5″ piece diagonally as a tulip stem on each block according to the pattern, pin and machine edge-stitch or use a decorative stitch to hold in place.

2. Trace 16 tulip flowers, 16 posies, 16 posy centers, and 32 tulip leaves onto the paper side of a piece of fusible web. Fuse each set of flower parts to the wrong side of its corresponding fabric and cut out all of the pieces. Working one block at a time, lay the flowers in their places and fuse according to manufacturer's directions. Machine satin stitch all raw edges using appropriate colors of thread for each appliqué. Press all of the blocks.

Assembling the Quilt

1. Refer to the following diagrams to stitch the blocks and sashing strips together, using accurate ¼″ seam allowances. Press the seams toward the sashing strips.

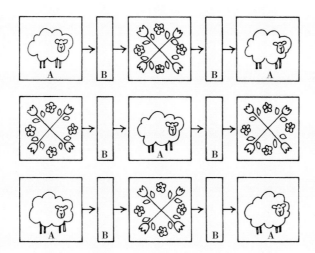

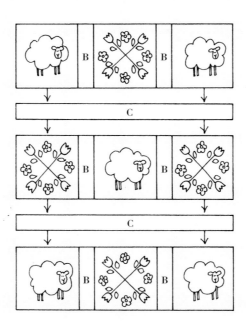

15

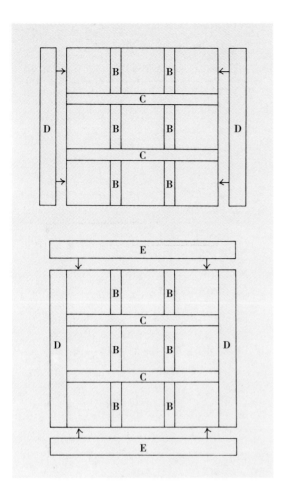

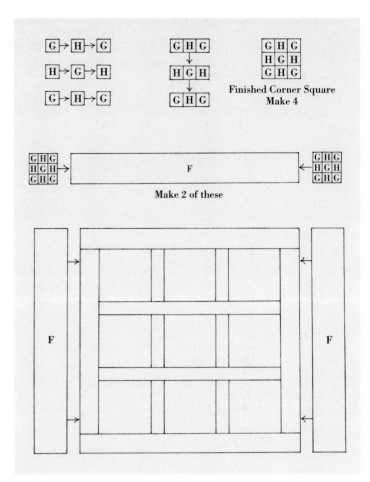

Finished Corner Square
Make 4

Make 2 of these

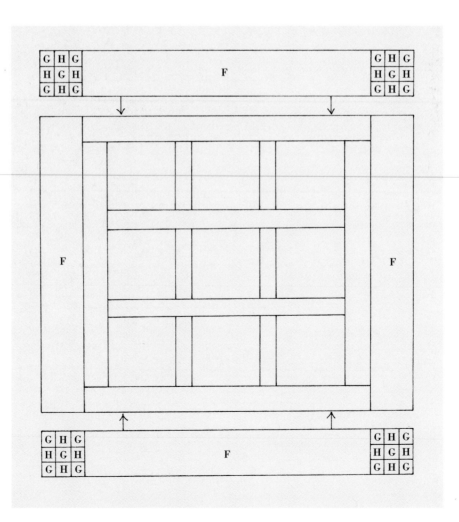

2. Once all the A through H blocks are sewn together, use the machine appliqué technique to apply the corner bow on the upper left corner of the border section of the quilt top. The section of the bow that goes down the side of the quilt is the mirror image of the section that goes across the top of the quilt, so you will need to trace one as shown and one as a mirror image to get the whole bow.

3. Press your quilt top.

4. The backing fabric must be at least 46″ wide. Many fabrics are available for quilt backing that are wider than 45″ just for this purpose. If you are using a 44″-wide fabric, you will need to stitch two lengths together to get the required width. Press the seam to one side.

5. Using a wash-out marking pen or pencil, mark the quilt top with a quilting design that you like. The designs used on this quilt are included here (page 96); see the photo for placement of each element. Backgrounds are done in a 1″ grid pattern. Make it as plain or as fancy as you wish.

6. Lay out the backing fabric right side down on a flat surface. It may help to tape the edges down to keep the fabric taut. Next, place a layer of batting and smooth out any bunched areas. Now lay out your quilt top, right side up. When everything is smooth, you can baste the layers together, starting from the center and working outward. There are lots of ways to baste a quilt, but my favorite is the old-fashioned way of using a needle and thread. I feel the control is better, and your quilting thread won't get hung up on any little pieces of hardware that other methods require. Your basting stitches should be 1″ to 2″ long and should cover the quilt at approximately 5″ intervals.

7. Now it's time to quilt. A quilting stitch is simply a running stitch that holds all the layers of the quilt together while making a design on the surface of the quilt. Some people like to put their quilts into quilting frames to do the actual quilting, while others just set the quilt on their lap. You decide which way works best for you. To begin a row of quilting, knot the end of the thread, take one stitch and pull the knot through the fabric so it is buried in the batting layer of the quilt.

8. When the quilting is done, you can bind the edges of your quilt. First trim the edges so the batting and backing are even with the quilt top. Then cut enough strips of 1½″ bias so that when they are stitched end-to-end they are about 190″ long. Press the joining seams all one direction. Fold the binding in half lengthwise, wrong sides together, matching the raw edges together. Press the whole length of it.

9. Pin the binding to the front side of the quilt, matching the raw edges. Miter the corners as you come to them. Stitch the binding to the quilt using an accurate ¼″ seam allowance. Wrap the folded edge of the binding around to the back side of the quilt and pin. Blind stitch in place.

10. If you plan to hang your quilt on the wall as decoration, you can sew a sleeve to the back to accommodate a curtain rod.

"Flowers for Ewe" Crib Bumpers

These bumpers were made to match the "Flowers for Ewe" quilt. They use an extra loft batting for cushioning and are made double width, then folded in half to make the most of the batting. The finished size fits a standard 27″ by 51″ crib.

MATERIALS

❦ 3 yards background fabric (ivory)
❦ ¾ yard sashing and binding fabric (pale pink)
❦ ¼ yard light gray (faces and legs)
❦ ½ yard fuzzy white fabric (lambs)
❦ ½ yard pale green (leaves, stems, and border squares)
❦ ¼ yard light pink (tulips)
❦ ¼ yard light blue (checkerboard sections)
❦ 1 yard paper-backed fusible web
❦ 3 yards white muslin for backing
❦ wash-out fabric marking pen or pencil
❦ black fine-point permanent fabric marking pen
❦ thread to match fabric colors
❦ dark gray thread (lamb hooves)
❦ ½″ bias tape maker (optional)
❦ twin-size extra-loft batting (72″ by 90″)
❦ quilter's safety pins for basting (optional)
❦ rotary cutter, cutting board, and ruler are very helpful, but not essential
❦ 5 skeins of embroidery floss for tying

INSTRUCTIONS

Note: Patterns are on pages 92–93. All seam allowances are ¼″ unless otherwise specified. The letters in parentheses indicate pieces as labeled on the assembly diagram. The colors are included in parentheses so you can see the relationship of colors to each other in the photograph and to clarify where each piece will go. You may wish to substitute other colors.

1. Wash, dry, and press all fabrics before cutting.
2. (A) Cut 8 squares 9½″ by 9½″ (ivory).
   (B) Cut 8 rectangles 4½″ by 9½″ (ivory).
   (C) Cut 4 rectangles 8½″ by 5½″ (ivory).
   (D) Cut 3 strips 1½″ by 44″ (ivory).
   (E) Cut 3 strips 1½″ by 44″ (light blue).
   (F) Cut 30 sashing strips 1½″ by 9½″ (pale pink).
   (G) Cut 16 sashing strips 1½″ by 4½″ (pale pink).
   (H) Cut 8 sashing strips 1½″ by 8½″ (pale pink).
   (I) Cut 42 border blocks 1½″ by 1½″ (pale green).
   (J) Cut 4 outer panels 12¼″ by 44″ (ivory).
   (K) Cut 4 backing panels 26″ by 44″ (white muslin).
   (L) Cut 6 binding strips 1½″ by 44″ (pale pink).
   (M) Cut 6 tie strips 2½″ by 21″ (ivory).
3. Make eight lamb blocks according to instructions in the "Flowers for Ewe" quilt (page 14) using the 9½″ by 9½″ (A) squares.

Tall Tulip Blocks

1. Make the stems first by cutting 64″ of 1″ pale green bias. Fold the long raw edges to the center and press or run it through a ½″ bias tape maker and press. Fold in half lengthwise again to make a ¼″-wide strip and press. Cut eight 4¾″ pieces. Find the vertical center of each of the eight ivory (4½″ by 9½″) rectangle (B) blocks by folding each in half. Place one 4¾″ length of bias on the center line having the lower raw edge 1⅜″ from the lower edge of the fabric. Pin and machine edge-stitch or use a decorative stitch to hold in place. Use a machine satin stitch and green thread to cover the lower raw edge of the stem (same technique as for the lambs' hooves, page 14).
2. Trace 20 tulip flowers and 32 leaves (page 93) onto the paper side of the fusible web. Fuse each set of flower parts to the wrong side of its corresponding fabric and cut out all the pieces. Lay one tulip flower on each stem and fuse according to manufacturer's directions. Repeat for leaves using the photograph as a guide for placement. Machine satin stitch all raw edges using appropriate colors of thread for each appliqué.

Checkerboard Tulip Blocks

1. Cut twelve 2″ long, pale green stems from the ¼″ folded bias previously made. Place three stems on each 8½″ by 5½″ (C) block, with 2¼″ between them. The stems should be 1″ from the bottom edge of the block. Pin and top stitch as before. Machine satin stitch the lower raw edge using green thread. Fuse and satin stitch a tulip and two leaves to each stem as before.
2. The following technique is called strip piecing and speeds up the piecing of quilt blocks. Using an accurate ¼″ seam allowance, stitch one (D) strip to one (E) strip, right sides together. Repeat for the other two sets of (D) and (E) strips. Press the seams toward the blue. Now, crosscut the strips into 1½″ sections. (Fig. 1) You will need 64 of these crosscut pieces. As you are cutting, make sure your cuts are exactly 90 degrees to the seam and that each piece is precisely 1½″ wide.

3. Lay one (D-E) unit over another, right sides together, but turn the top one 180 degrees around so its blue is over the ivory of the bottom piece. Match the center seams, keeping the raw edges even, and stitch an accurate ¼″ seam. You can feed these pairs of (D-E) units through the sewing machine one right after another and then cut them apart after all 32 pairs are stitched. Press each four-square block open. Now repeat the process to join the four-square blocks to each other to make sixteen 8-square blocks. And then again to make eight 16-square checkerboard strips. Be sure to keep the raw edges even and seam allowances accurate at ¼″ as you work. Press the seams all in one direction.

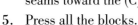

Fig. 1

4. Pin one checkerboard strip to the top of each (C) block, matching raw edges and corners carefully. Stitch an accurate ¼″ seam. Pin and stitch the remaining four checkerboard strips to the bottom edges of these blocks. Press seams toward the (C) block.

Fig. 2

5. Press all the blocks.

6. Stitch an (F) sashing strip to the right-hand side of each (A) lamb, (B) tall tulip, and (C) checkerboard tulip block. (Fig. 2)

7. Refer to the following diagrams to stitch the blocks and sashing strips together using accurate ¼″ seams. (Figs. 3 and 4) Press the seam allowances toward the sashing strips.

8. Stitch a 1½″ by 1½″ sashing block (I) to one end of each of the remaining (F), (G), and (H) sashing strips. (Fig. 5)

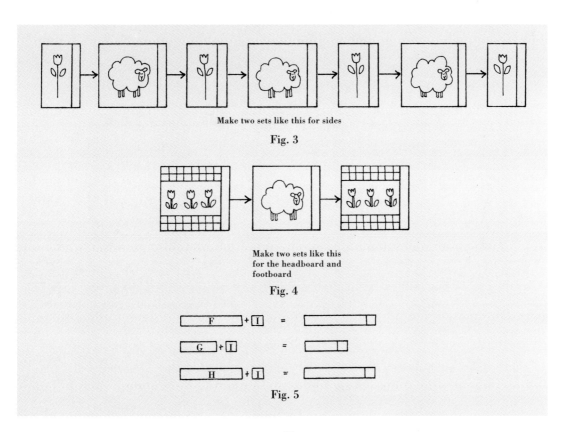

Make two sets like this for sides

Fig. 3

Make two sets like this for the headboard and footboard

Fig. 4

Fig. 5

21

9. Lay out the bumper sections, one at a time, on a flat surface and lay out the sashing strip and block units to correspond with the block it will be attached to. The (A) lamb blocks fit to the (F) sashing strips, the (B) tall tulip blocks fit to the (G) sashing strips, and the (C) checkerboard tulip blocks fit to the (H) sashing strips. When the strips are in the right order, stitch them end-to-end to make a long strip. Press all the seams in one direction. You will need four strips to fit the side bumper sections and four strips to fit the headboard and footboard bumper sections.

10. Pin one (G-I-F...) sashing and block combination strip to the top and bottom of each bumper side panel, matching raw edges and seams. Stitch an accurate ¼″ seam.

11. Pin one (H-I-F...) sashing and block combination strip to the top and bottom of each headboard and footboard panel, matching raw edges and seams. Stitch an accurate ¼″ seam.

12. Stitch the panels together, end-to-end, in the following order: footboard + side + headboard + side to make one very long panel. Press the seams toward the sashing strips.

13. Stitch the four (J) outer panels end-to-end to make one very long panel (12¼″ by 175″). Press the seams all in one direction.

14. With right sides together, pin the outer panel to the quilt block panel along the bottom edge. Stitch an accurate ¼″ seam. Trim off the excess outer panel fabric. Press the seam toward the outer panel.

15. Stitch the backing panels (K) end-to-end to make one very long panel (26″ by 175″). Press the seams all in one direction.

16. To layer and baste this project, a long table is very helpful, but you will still have to work in sections. Lay out the backing, wrong side up. It may help to tape the edges to the table to keep the fabric taut. Then, cut a length of extra-loft batting 26″ by the length of the batting. Lay this over the backing and smooth out any bunched areas. Then, lay the quilt block section on top, centering it over the backing, which is slightly wider than the top section to allow for error. The extra will be trimmed off later. You will need to add another length of batting as you progress down the length of the bumpers. Simply butt the edges together and loosely whipstitch the batting sections to each other, then continue the layering and basting process. To baste the layers together in this project, I used lots of quilter's safety pins, pinning the layers together about every 5″. If you plan to quilt your bumpers, you may want to baste with thread as for the "Flowers for Ewe" quilt. But for the quicker tying method, the safety pins work fine.

17. When the entire length is pinned, use a machine straight stitch to "stitch in the ditch" of the long center seam that joins the outer panel and quilt block panel. Then, stitch again parallel to that row but ¾″ into the outer panel. These stitching lines will become the fold lines.

18. Lay the bumpers out again on a flat surface and use the embroidery floss to tie the layers together. This means you will cut a length of embroidery floss (about 36″) and thread it into a needle (a size 5 or 7 crewel needle works well). Take a single stitch, catching all three layers, and tie a knot at that point. Cut off the thread ends about ½″ above the knot. Continue tying these knots about every 4″ or 5″ over the surface of the bumpers. I lined up my knots with the sashing strips and centers of the blocks. This

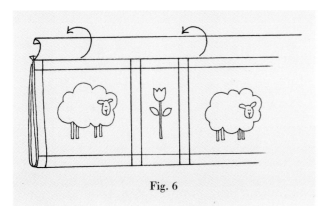

Fig. 6

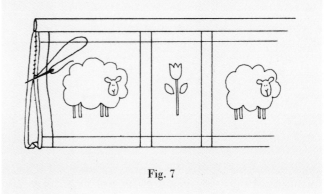

Fig. 7

job may seem as though it will take an eternity, but it will probably take about three hours.

19. Hand-baste ¼″ in from the edges with thread all the way around to make the binding process easier.

20. Fold one long edge over ¼″ on two binding strips (L) and press. Pin one binding strip (L), right sides together and matching raw edges, to each of the short sides of the bumpers. Stitch an accurate ¼″ seam. Wrap the folded edge of the binding around to the back side of the bumpers and blind stitch in place.

21. Stitch four of the binding strips (L) end-to-end to make one very long strip. Press the seams in one direction. Fold over one long edge ¼″ down the length of the strip and press. Place the binding strip right sides together to the upper edge of the quilt block side of the bumpers. Keeping the raw edges even, stitch an accurate ¼″ seam. There is no need to pin this before stitching as you will have to remove the pins because the fabric will creep under the foot of the machine and pins will only encourage unwanted tucks. Trim off the extra binding.

22. Fold the bumpers right side out, matching corners and raw edges. Wrap the folded edge of the binding around to the outer panel side of the bumpers. (Fig. 6) Pin and blind stitch in place.

23. Blind stitch the open ends of the bumpers together to close the opening. (Fig. 7)

24. Fold the tie strips (M) right sides together, lengthwise, keeping the raw edges even. Stitch across one end, then pivot at the corner and stitch down the long raw edge. Repeat for all tie strips. Clip extra fabric from corners and turn right side out. Press well, turning in the raw edge at the same time. Stitch the turned-in edge closed.

25. Cut *one* tie in half to make two ties about 10″ long each. Turn in the raw edges and finger press. Pin one of these half ties to the top of each of the outer panel corners. Stitch in place.

26. Fold the other five ties in half to find the centers. Pin the center of each tie to the upper edge of the outer panel at what will be the corners and side centers. Stitch in place.

Mobile

MATERIALS

❖ ¼ yard white fuzzy fabric

❖ ⅛ yard gray cotton fabric

❖ ⅜ yard cotton fabric for hoop cover and ruffle

❖ 15″ by 20″ sheet of mat board

❖ 2½ yards of ¼″-wide ribbon

❖ 1 yard of 1″-wide ribbon

❖ 2 yards of 1″-wide ribbon for the bow at the top

❖ inside ring of a 12″ round quilting hoop

❖ small saw

❖ tape

❖ tacky glue

❖ 2½ yards of white cording

❖ X-acto® or craft knife

❖ 16″ by 16″ remnant of batting

❖ black fine-point permanent fabric marking pen or paint writer

INSTRUCTIONS

Note: Pattern is on page 97.

Hoop

1. Cut one 3½″ by 39″ strip of fabric for the hoop cover. Cut two 4″ by 45″ strips of fabric for the ruffle.

2. Stitch the two ruffle strips end-to-end to make one long strip and press the seam open. Fold the ruffle strip wrong sides together, matching the raw edges down the length of the strip.

3. Run two rows of gathering stitches ⅛″ and ⅜″ in from the raw edges. Fold the ends of the hoop cover under ¼″ and press. Find the center of the hoop cover strip and the center of the ruffle. Pin the centers together, matching the raw edges. Pin the ends, matching the raw edges. (Fig. 1)

4. Pull up the gathering threads and adjust the gathers to fit the hoop cover. Pin and stitch in place. Press the ruffles outward.

5. Fold the opposite long raw edge of the hoop cover under ¼″ and press.

6. Fold the hoop cover in half lengthwise, matching the long folded edge to the seam of the ruffle edge. Pin and blind stitch in place. (Fig. 2)

7. Using a small saw, make a cut through the hoop and slip the hoop cover onto the hoop. With the hoop cover pushed back a few inches, tape the cut edges back together. Slide the ends of the hoop cover together so they meet and blind stitch the ends together.

Lambs

1. Using the patterns provided, trace five lamb shapes and five mirror-image lamb shapes onto the mat board on the mat cutting line. Carefully cut out the shapes with an X-acto® or craft knife.
2. Glue a layer of batting to the right side of each mat board lamb shape. Trim the batting around the curves.
3. Using the pattern provided, cut five lamb shapes and five mirror-image lamb shapes from the fuzzy white fabric on the fabric cutting line.
4. Lay one batting-covered mat shape facedown on the wrong side of one corresponding lamb fabric piece. Clip into corners and curves. (Fig. 3)
5. Dab some glue on the back edges of the mat lamb shape and wrap the turning allowance to the back and into the glue. Work your way around the shape, gluing and wrapping until the lamb shape is covered smoothly. Repeat for all ten shapes.
6. For legs cut a 1″ wide by 30″ long strip of gray fabric. Fold it right sides together and stitch a ¼″ seam the length of it. Mark the strip at 1½″ intervals and stitch across the strip at those intervals. (Fig. 4) Cut the strip into 20 pieces ⅛″ above the stitching lines. Turn each right side out and press.
7. Place four of the legs on the wrong side of each of the five covered lamb shapes, having the raw edge of each leg approximately ½″ into the lower edge. (Fig. 5) Glue each leg in place.
8. Cut four 7″ lengths and one 12″ length of ¼″ ribbon (the longer one is for the lamb that hangs in the center of the mobile). Glue the end of one ribbon to the top of each covered lamb. (Fig. 5)
9. Glue one mirror-image lamb shape to each corresponding lamb shape, wrong sides together. The tops of the legs and ribbon end will be sandwiched in between.
10. Glue cording around each lamb shape over the joint between the front and back.
11. Cut five lamb faces from the gray felt. Draw the faces on using black permanent fabric marking pen or paint writer, and let dry. Glue one lamb head to each lamb body as desired.

Assembly

1. Cut two 18″ lengths of 1″ ribbon and turn the raw ends of each ribbon to the outside ¼″ and stitch.
2. Mark the center of each ribbon by folding and pressing with your fingers. Lay one ribbon on the other at a 90-degree angle, matching the centers. Pin and stitch them together. (Fig. 6)
3. Cut a 48″ length of ¼″ ribbon. Turn one end under twice and stitch the turned-under end to the center of the crossed ribbons.
4. On the covered hoop, mark quarter intervals around the top edge (Fig. 7). Stitch the ends of the crossed ribbons to the hoop covering at those intervals.

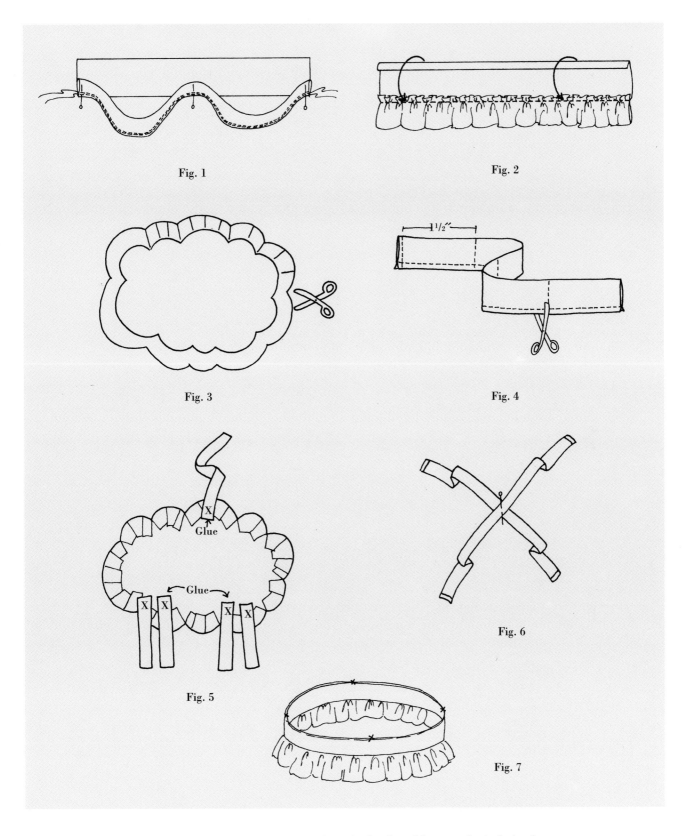

Fig. 1

Fig. 2

Fig. 3

Fig. 4

Fig. 5

Fig. 6

Fig. 7

5. Turn under the raw edge of each of the lamb's ribbons and stitch the four shorter ones at the quarter intervals around the inside of the covered hoop. You can have them all the same length or vary them a bit. Stitch the longer lamb's ribbon to the center of the crossed ribbons.

6. Using a 1″-wide ribbon, make a fluffy bow with several loops, stitched together at the center. Stitch the fluffy bow to the crossed ribbons at the base of the hanger ribbon.

7. Hang the mobile from a hook in the ceiling.

Lampshade

MATERIALS

❖ 1 smooth lampshade, any size

❖ paper

❖ pencil

❖ 1 yard of fabric (this will accommodate all but the largest shades)

❖ fabric or acrylic paints: white, light gray, light pink, light green

❖ soft artist's paintbrush

❖ thin-bodied tacky glue

❖ fine-point permanent marking pen

❖ trims (lace, cord, braid, or fringe) as you like, amount determined by the size of your shade

INSTRUCTIONS

1. Smoothly cover your lampshade with paper, taping as necessary. Trim the excess paper, as close as possible, to the top and bottom edge of the shade. (Fig. 1)

2. Remove the paper from the shade. This will be your pattern.

3. Press the fabric so it is very smooth. Transfer the pattern shape to the fabric adding 1″ on all sides. (Fig. 2) Cut out.

4. Trace the lamb designs on page 98 onto the shade fabric using a pencil and a light touch.

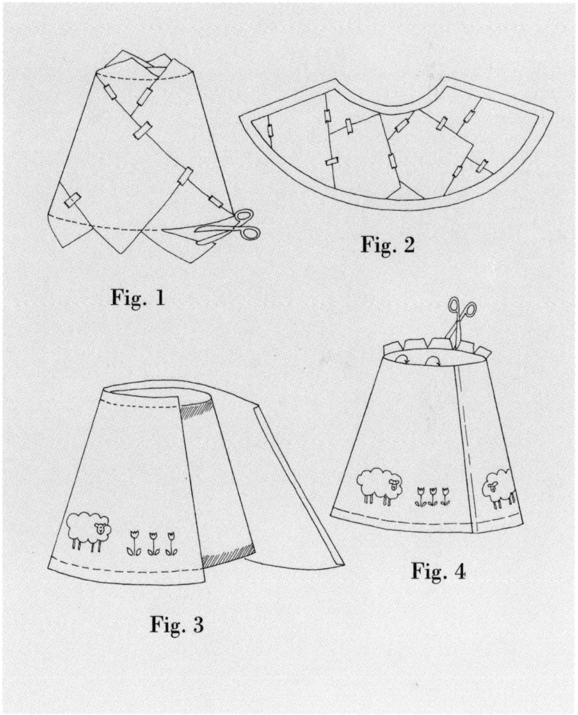

5. Paint in the designs as desired and let dry completely. Press to set the colors. Add the lamb faces using a fine-point permanent marking pen.

6. Spread a very thin layer of tacky glue around the top and bottom 1″ of the shade. Carefully lay the shade cover on, being careful not to stretch it as you gently smooth it into place. (Fig. 3)

7. Once the cover is smooth, turn the back edge under about ½″ and glue down. Trim the top and bottom edges to about ½″ and make clips into the top edge as necessary to make it fold over the top and lay smoothly to the inside. Glue in place. (Fig. 4)

8. Turn the bottom edge to the inside and glue in place.

9. Trim with lace, cord, braid, or fringe, as desired.

Fig. 1

Fig. 2

Fig. 3

Fig. 4

Things to Wear

Hats

Baby Cap

MATERIALS

❧ ¼ yard of cotton knit (if you want two coordinating fabrics as shown
in the photo, you will need ¼ yard of each)

❧ thread

INSTRUCTIONS

Note: All seam allowances are ¼″.

1. Using the pattern provided (page 99), cut one baby cap on the fold of the
    fabric. Cut one of cotton knit lining fabric.

2. Fold baby cap, right sides together, matching raw edges. Pin and stitch as
    shown. (Fig. 1) Repeat for the cap lining, but leave a 2″ opening in the
    center back seam as shown. (Fig. 2)

3. Refold the baby cap as shown, bringing previously sewn seams together.
    Pin and stitch across the top of the cap. (Fig. 3) Repeat for the cap lining.

4. Place the baby cap and cap lining right sides together, matching the back
    seams and the lower raw edges of the cap and lining. Pin and stitch all
    the way around the lower edge (Fig. 4), stretching slightly as you stitch.

5. Turn right side out through the opening in the back seam of the lining.
    Press the lower edges and slip stitch the opening in the cap lining.

6. Turn up the lower edge so lining shows on the outside.

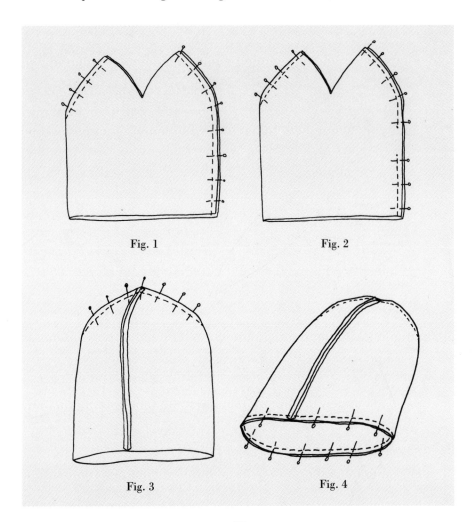

Fig. 1   Fig. 2

Fig. 3   Fig. 4

Winter Hats

MATERIALS

- ♣ ¼ yard of corduroy or velveteen
- ♣ ¼ yard of fleece or imitation fur
- ♣ thread
- ♣ ¾ yard of ½″ single-fold bias tape in a color to match hat
- ♣ 3 buttons (for boy's hat)
- ♣ 3 tiny appliqués and ½ yard of ¼″ ribbon (for girl's hat)

INSTRUCTIONS

1. Cut two hat sections of velveteen or corduroy, using patterns on pages 100–101. Cut two hat sections of fleece or imitation fur for lining.
2. Stitch darts in each hat section, including lining sections. (Fig. 1)
3. Place hat sections right sides together, matching front and back seams. Stitch a ¼″ seam. Repeat for the lining. (Fig. 2)
4. Cut two brim sections or one ruffle section of fleece or imitation fur (pattern on page 101). For boys' hat trim, place right sides together. Pin and stitch the longer curved edge. Clip seam around stitched curve (Fig. 3) and turn right side out. Press and baste raw edges together.
5. For brim (boys), find center of brim section and pin to center front of hat section, matching raw edges. Baste in place. For ruffle (girls), fold wrong sides together and run two lines of gathering threads along raw edges. Find center of ruffle and pin to center front of hat section. Pull up gathers to 4″ on each side of center. Pin and baste in place. (Fig. 4)
6. Fold bias tape in half lengthwise to ¼″ wide. Stitch the entire length of it. Pin and stitch ends of bias to hat as shown. (Fig. 4)
7. With right sides together, pin lining to hat, matching center front and back seams, keeping the ties out of the stitching line.
8. Stitch around hat edges, leaving a 4″ opening at the back of the neck edge for turning. Clip curves. Turn right side out and press.
9. Fold under raw edges at back of neck opening and slip-stitch closed.
10. Topstitch around all edges ¼″ from edges.
11. For boy's hat, turn brim back and tack in place or use a button (well-secured) for decoration. For girl's hat, stitch on tiny appliqués as desired and a bow at the top center where the seams all come together.

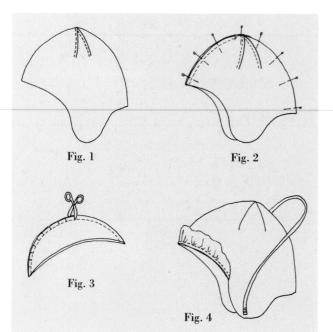

Fig. 1   Fig. 2

Fig. 3

Fig. 4

Sun Hat

MATERIALS

❖ ¼ yard cotton fabric or scraps of 6 or 7 colors
❖ ¼ yard lining fabric (can be same as above)
❖ thread to match
❖ button, bow, or tiny appliqué (optional)

INSTRUCTIONS

1. Cut six sun hat crown sections according to pattern on page 102 from cotton fabric or scraps. Cut six crown sections from the lining fabric. Cut one 3″ by 28″ strip for the hat brim.

2. Pin two crown sections together and stitch a ¼″ seam (Fig. 1) from ⊕ at the top point to the lower edge. Add another crown section; pin and stitch from the ⊕ to the lower edge. Repeat for the remaining three crown sections so you have two 3-piece sections.

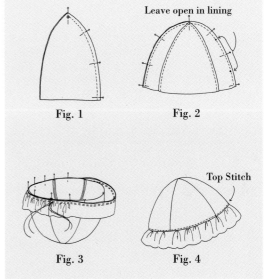

Fig. 1   Fig. 2

Leave open in lining

Fig. 3   Fig. 4

Top Stitch

3. Pin the two 3-piece crown sections together, matching raw edges, top points, and lower edges. Pin and stitch a ¼″ seam from the lower edge to the top point and back down to the opposite lower edge. (Fig. 2)

4. Repeat the above process to assemble the crown lining pieces, leaving a 2″ opening in one seam. (Fig. 2)

5. Fold the brim strip, right sides together, so the end raw edges match. Stitch a ¼″ seam across the ends.

6. Fold the brim wrong sides together, matching the raw edges, and press.

7. Run two rows of machine gathering threads ⅛″ and ⅜″ from the raw edge around the whole brim.

8. Mark the center of the brim (opposite the seam) and pin to the crown, matching the brim center to the center front of the crown and matching the brim seam to the center back of the crown. (Fig. 3) Pull up the bobbin threads to gather the brim fabric to fit the crown, matching the raw edges. Pin and baste in place.

9. Pin the lining to the crown, right sides together (brim will be between the layers), matching the center front and center back seams. Stitch a ¼″ seam.

10. Turn the hat right side out through the opening in the lining. Slip stitch the opening closed.

11. Topstitch around the crown, just above the brim. (Fig. 4)

12. Add a button, bow, or tiny appliqué to the top of the crown and secure well.

Monogram Bib

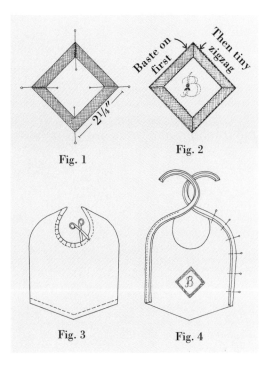

Fig. 1

Fig. 2

Fig. 3

Fig. 4

MATERIALS

❦ scrap of white batiste for monogram

❦ wash-out marking pen or pencil

❦ embroidery floss (your choice of colors for monogram)

❦ 12″ of ⅜″ insertion lace

❦ glass head pins

❦ ¼ yard of fabric

❦ 1¾ yards of narrow bias binding (¼″ double folded)
   or ½ yard of fabric to cut bias from

❦ 12″ of ⅝″ lace edging with beading

❦ 12″ of ¼″ ribbon

INSTRUCTIONS

1. Work monogram (see alphabet on page 103) on a scrap of white batiste fabric using a shadow embroidery stitch (see Stitch Reference for help with working the stitches). Mark a 1½″ diamond around monogram with wash-out marker or pencil.

2. Make a diamond of ⅜″ insertion lace with an outside measurement of 2¼″ and an inside measurement of 1½″ by pinning the lace, using glass head pins, at each outer point to your ironing board. (Fig. 1) Press, then tiny zigzag stitch each corner.

3. Layer monogram over a piece of white fabric. Place the lace diamond on the marked shape around the monogram.

4. Hand baste all three layers together.

5. Tiny zigzag stitch or hand pinstitch the inside edge of the lace to the fabrics. Carefully trim extra fabric from behind the lace.

6. Using the pattern given, page 102, cut two bib sections from fabric.

7. Pin the monogram diamond to one layer of bib center front. Baste, then tiny zigzag or hand pinstitch in place around outer edges of lace insertion. (Fig. 2)

8. Place both bib sections right sides together, stitch around neck edge and lower edge. Clip curves and corners. Turn right side out and press. (Fig. 3)

9. Cut two strips of bias 1″ wide by 23″ long. Press the long edges to meet in the center, or use a ½″ bias tape maker. You can use premade ½″ single-fold bias tape, if desired.

10. Stitch bias to each side of the bib having raw edges even and leaving long tails at neck edge for ties. (Fig. 4)

11. Turn the folded edge of the bias to the back side and blind stitch in place. Fold and stitch the length of the ties, too. Knot the ends of the ties.

12. Thread ¼″ ribbon through the beading holes of the lace edging. Pin to the lower edge of the bib and miter the corner. Press. Unpin and stitch the mitered corner.

13. Pin the lace to the bib front at the lower edge and turn the raw edges of the lace under and pin. Topstitch the lace in place.

14. Wash out the marker or pencil lines.

Quilted and Appliquéd Bibs

MATERIALS

❦ ⅜ yard of cotton broadcloth

❦ wash-out marking pen or pencil

❦ remnant (9″ by 12″) of white cotton batting

❦ needle

❦ quilting thread

❦ sewing thread

INSTRUCTIONS

1. Using a wash-out marking pen, transfer the bib design to the fabric by tracing. Patterns are on pages 104–105.

2. Layer one piece of fabric, one piece of cotton batting, and the second piece of fabric with the traced quilting design. Pin through all three layers and quilt by hand (see Stitch Reference) or machine.

3. Cut 60″ of 1″ bias strips from leftover fabric. Stitch end-to-end using ¼″ seams to make one long strip. Fold and press both long edges to the center (a bias tape maker is helpful here) or use purchased single-fold bias tape.

4. To bind the neck edge of the bib, match the raw edge of the bias strip to the raw edge of the bib; pin and stitch. (Fig. 1) If you press the bias strip into a curved shape before pinning, this will go more smoothly.

5. Trim seam to ³⁄₁₆″ and clip curves. (Fig. 2)

6. Turn the folded edge of the bias to the back side of the bib; pin and blind stitch in place. (Fig. 3)

7. Fold a 48″ strip of bias tape in half to find the center. Pin to the center lower edge of the bib, right sides together, working first to one side then to the other, leaving tails at the top neck edge. (Fig. 4)

8. Turn the folded edge of the bias to the back side of the bib; pin and blind stitch in place. Continue blind stitching on tails to make ties.

9. Knot the ends of ties and rinse out marker ink with plain water.

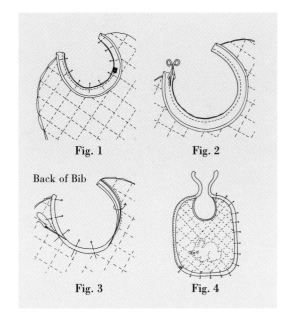

Fig. 1 Fig. 2

Back of Bib

Fig. 3 Fig. 4

Note: For appliquéd bib, use appliqué designs for Cozy Blankets (page 90), following appliqué instructions on page 9 before layering and quilting. Then proceed as above.

Little Boots

Bunny Boots

MATERIALS

- ♣ ¼ yard of white velour
- ♣ ¼ yard of pink cotton for lining
- ♣ thread
- ♣ pink embroidery floss
- ♣ 2 tiny black buttons or embroidery floss for eyes
- ♣ 1 yard of ¼″ ribbon

INSTRUCTIONS

Note: Patterns are on page 106.

1. To make the ears, layer one ear and one ear lining section right sides together. Pin and stitch around ear, leaving the bottom edge open for turning. Fold tucks into each ear as indicated on the pattern piece and baste.

2. With right sides together, stitch the center front seam on the upper boot section. Repeat for the upper boot lining sections. (Fig. 1)

3. Pin the lining to the upper boot section at the upper edge, right sides together and matching front seams. Stitch the upper edge. (Fig. 2) Turn right side out.

4. Place ears, one to each side of the center seam of the upper boot section, matching lower raw edges of upper boot section to raw edges of ear sections. Pin, then baste around the lower edge of upper boot, including ears. (Fig. 3)

5. Pin toe lining to boot toe, wrong sides together. Baste around all edges.

6. Pin toe to upper boot section, right sides together, matching centers and corners. (Fig. 4) Stitch.

7. Embroider bunny nose using two strands of pink floss and a satin stitch (see Stitch Reference).

8. Place eyes (I used tiny buttons and secured them well), or embroider using six strands of floss and French knots.

9. Pin the sole to the sole lining, wrong sides together, and baste all edges.

10. Pin the sole to the boot, matching center fronts and center backs. Stitch and turn right side out.

11. Cut an 18″ length of ¼″ ribbon and knot the ends. Find the center of the ribbon and pin to the center back of the boot, ¾″ above heel seam. Hand stitch in place.

12. Tack the ears to each other and to the upper part of the boot.

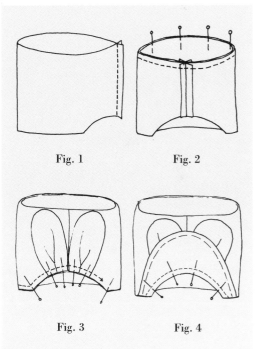

Fig. 1   Fig. 2

Fig. 3   Fig. 4

Baby Shoes

MATERIALS

* ⅓ yard cotton outer fabric
* ¼ yard cotton flannel
* ¼ yard paper-backed fusible web
* thread
* ½″ bias tape maker (optional but very helpful)
* awl
* 4 small grommets and attaching tool (optional)
* 24″ of ribbon for shoe ties

INSTRUCTIONS

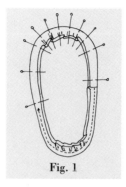

Fig. 1

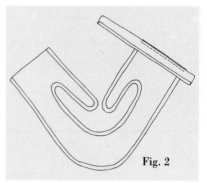

Fig. 2

1. Cut a 9″ by 20″ piece each of the cotton outer fabric, flannel, and fusible web. Following manufacturer's directions, fuse the flannel to the wrong side of the cotton outer fabric.

2. Using the patterns given (page 107), cut two baby shoe uppers and two soles from the fused fabric.

3. Cut six strips of 1″ bias from the leftover outer fabric (each one should be about 16″ long). On each piece, fold the long raw edges to the center and press or run them through a ½″ bias tape maker and press.

4. To bind the edges of each sole, unfold and match the long raw edge of one bias strip to the raw edge of the sole, beginning at the side. Pin (every ¼″ around the toe and heel), then stitch by machine using a ¼″ seam. Turn the folded edge to the flannel side of the sole and blindstitch in place. Repeat for both soles (Fig. 1).

5. Using the binding process above, bind all but the center back edges of the uppers. It is easier to hand baste instead of pinning the binding when working on the tight curves of the strap areas.

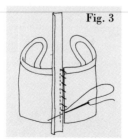

Fig. 3

6. With right sides together, pin a 4″-long piece of binding to one center back edge of each shoe upper, matching the raw edge of the binding to the raw edge of the center back and leaving ½″ tail to the lower edge and 1¾″ to the top edge. (Fig. 2)

7. Butt the center back edges together and whipstitch to hold. (Fig. 3) Lay the binding (which is stitched down on one edge) over the joint and pin the folded edge to the opposite side of the center back of the shoe. (Fig. 4) Fold the binding tails to the inside of the shoe, turning under the raw edge. Blind stitch in place.

8. Pin the sole to the shoe upper, matching center front and center back, and blind stitch the bound edges together.

9. Use an awl to make a hole in the end of each strap and hand buttonhole stitch the edges. Or use a grommet tool and attach a grommet to each strap end.

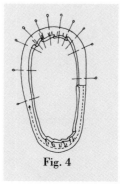

Fig. 4

10. Thread a 12″ length of ribbon through the holes in each ankle strap and tie.

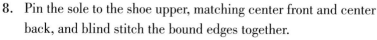

Booties

MATERIALS
❧ wash-out marking pen
❧ ¼ yard of cotton for outside
❧ ¼ yard of flannel for lining
❧ thread
❧ 1¼ yards of ½″ ribbon

INSTRUCTIONS

1. Cut out pieces as indicated on patterns (page 108). Using wash-out marker, mark the buttonholes and casing lines as indicated on the patterns.

2. Stay-stitch the inner curve of the bootie upper. Clip to the stitching line about every ¼″ around the curve. (Fig. 1) Repeat for linings.

3. Pin the stay-stitched edge of the bootie upper to the bootie front panel, stretching the clipped and curved edge of the bootie upper to fit around the opposite curve of the bootie front panel. (Fig. 2) You will need to pin this about every ¼″. Carefully stitch around the pinned curve, removing the pins as you go. Repeat for linings.

4. Press seam toward bootie upper. On the right side, edge-stitch around the curve of the bootie upper, catching the seam allowance on the under side. Repeat for linings.

5. Make two ½″ buttonholes in the bootie center panel as indicated on the pattern piece.

6. With right sides together, stitch the back seam of the bootie. Repeat for back seam of bootie lining, leaving a 1½″ opening for turning. (Fig. 3)

7. Pin the sole to the lower edge of the bootie upper, matching the center fronts and backs. (Fig. 4) Stitch. Repeat for linings.

8. With right sides together, pin the lining to the bootie at the upper edges. Stitch. Turn right side out through the opening in the back seam of the lining.

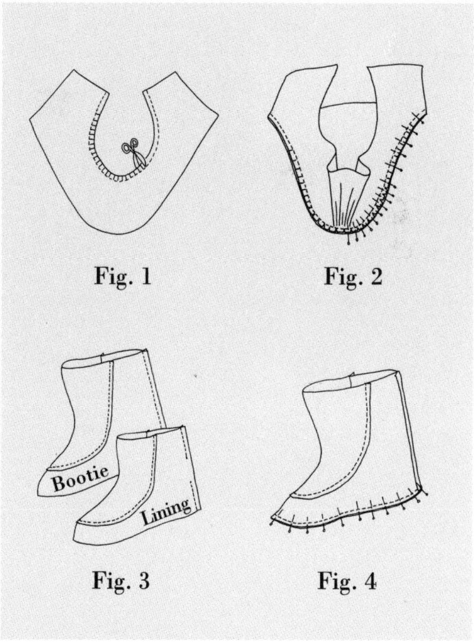

9. Press the upper edge. Slip stitch the opening in the back seam of the lining.

10. Turn the bootie inside out and pin inside at the casing marks. Stitch on the casing lines (two rows). **Note:** If you are hand stitching the casing lines, the bootie can be right side out.

11. Turn right side out and thread a 24″ length of ½″ ribbon through the casing by attaching a safety pin to one end of the ribbon and easing it through.

Fig. 1

Fig. 2

Fig. 3

Fig. 4

Bootie

Lining

Sock Bunnies

This cute bunny toy is a very good project for a beginning needle artist. It is approximately 13″ tall when finished and can be machine washed and dried.

MATERIALS

❖ 1 pair of tube socks (adult-size)
❖ wash-out marking pen
❖ thread
❖ stuffing
❖ pink embroidery floss
❖ 2 tiny black ball buttons or black embroidery floss for eyes
❖ 11″ by 25″ remnant for bunny suit
❖ 15″ of flat eyelet trim for a collar (optional)
❖ 15″ of ribbon (optional)
❖ tiny safety pin

INSTRUCTIONS

1. Turn the socks inside out. On one sock, mark the bunny's ears and lower cutting line. On the second sock, mark the arms and legs as shown on the diagram on page 49.
2. Stitch both socks on the marked lines, leaving the lower straight edge of each arm and leg open.
3. On the first sock, cut around the ears leaving a ⅛″ seam allowance and then carefully cut between the ears to the pivot point of the stitching. Cut the sock straight across at the lower cutting line as indicated on the diagram.
4. On the second sock, cut out the arms and legs leaving a ⅛″ seam allowance.
5. Turn all the pieces right side out.
6. Hand stitch the base of each ear, pulling the thread snugly to gather.
7. Stuff the head lightly and hand stitch the neckline, pulling the threads in snugly.
8. Stuff the body a little more firmly than the head. Stuff the hands and feet. Run a hand-gathering stitch around each wrist and ankle, pulling the thread in to emphasize the hands and feet. Tie off the thread. Then stuff each arm and leg lightly.

9. Pin the legs to the front layer of the lower edge of the body (Fig. 1), matching the raw edges and having the seams to the middle. Stitch the legs on, then turn all the raw edges to the inside. Pin and stitch the lower edge of the body closed.

10. Turn the raw edges of each arm to the inside and pin to the body sides at the shoulders. Hand stitch each to the body, securing well.

11. Embroider the bunny's nose using two strands of pink floss and a satin stitch. Stitch the button eyes in place, securing very well, or use black floss and French knots for eyes.

Bunny Suit

1. Cut two bunny suit pieces and one neck facing piece from the fabric remnant according to the patterns on page 109.

2. Place the bunny suit pieces right sides together and stitch a ¼″ seam on each shoulder. Press the seams open.

3. Lay the neck facing piece on the neck opening of the bunny suit, right sides together. Pin and stitch the neck opening, clip the corners and curves, and cut on the center front line to the pivot point of the stitching. (Fig. 2)

4. Turn the facing to the inside and press. On the right side, topstitch around the neck opening.

5. Turn the edge of each sleeve under ¼″ and stitch.

6. Fold the bunny suit right sides together, matching the raw edges. Pin and stitch a ¼″ seam continuously from each sleeve edge down the side seam.

7. Turn the lower raw edge of each leg under ¼″ and stitch.

8. Fold the bunny suit right sides together again and stitch the inner leg seams. (Fig. 3)

9. Slip the bunny into the suit through the neck opening, then stitch the corners of the neck opening together.

10. Run a hand-gathering stitch around each sleeve and ankle edge of the suit and pull the thread tight so the sleeve and ankle edges are held in place. (Fig. 4)

11. Fold the ends of the flat eyelet trim under ¼″ and stitch. Fold the top edge under ⅜″ down the length of the strip and press. Stitch a seam ¼″ from the folded edge to form a casing. To thread the ¼″ ribbon through the casing, attach a tiny safety pin to the end of the ribbon and ease it through. Remove the safety pin.

12. Gather the lace collar on the ribbon and tie it around the bunny's neck. Knot the raw ends of the ribbon and trim off the excess.

13. Tack the collar and bow in place.

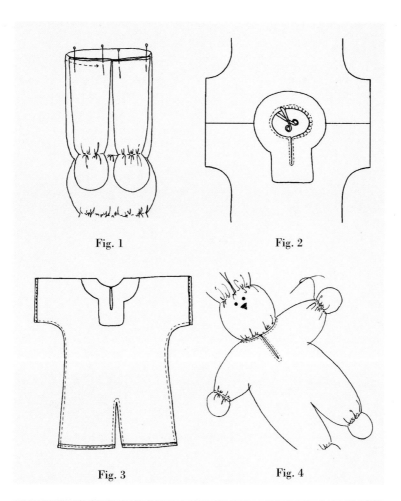

Fig. 1   Fig. 2

Fig. 3   Fig. 4

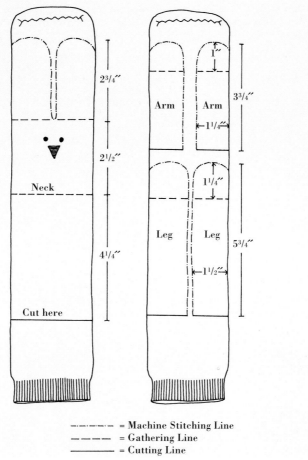

2³/₄″

2¹/₂″

Neck

4¹/₄″

Cut here

1″

Arm Arm

3³/₄″

1¹/₄″

1¹/₄″

Leg Leg

5³/₄″

1¹/₂″

—·—·—· = Machine Stitching Line

– – – – – = Gathering Line

————— = Cutting Line

Bear Rattle

MATERIALS

- ❧ 7″ by 14″ remnant of velour
- ❧ ¼ yard of cotton print for collar
- ❧ wash-out marking pen or pencil
- ❧ embroidery floss for nose and mouth
- ❧ 2 small round ball buttons for eyes
- ❧ plastic bubble from a gum ball machine
- ❧ 2 tiny jingle bells
- ❧ ½″ by 6″ dowel
- ❧ stuffing

INSTRUCTIONS

1. Cut out the pieces as indicated on the patterns (on page 110) and mark eye, nose and mouth placement.

2. With right sides together, stitch around bear ears as shown. (Fig. 1) Turn right side out. Make a small tuck in each ear as the pattern indicates and tack in place. (Fig. 1) The lower edge of the ear has a ½″ seam allowance to make this easier to do.

3. Place the ear on the dart seam of the head, face down, as shown. The extra ¼″ seam allowance should extend ¼″ past the raw edge of the dart seam. (Fig. 2)

4. Fold the back of the bear head over to match up both raw edges of the dart seam and sandwich the ear between the layers. Stitch the dart seam. (Fig. 2) Repeat for both head sections.

5. Pin head sections, right sides together, and stitch from back of neck around head to front of neck as shown. (Fig. 3)

6. Turn right side out. Stuff the head, adding in the jingle bells encased in the plastic gum ball machine bubble toward the nose section, making sure the plastic bubble is well padded.

7. Run a hand-gathering stitch around the neck edge and pull up very tightly to close the neck edge. Tie off.

8. Thread a needle with double quilting thread and knot the end. Insert needle into one eye marking and out at the other eye marking. Slip a small round eye button onto the needle, reinsert the needle a couple of threads away from where thread comes out, and have needle come out at

the first eye marking. Add the second eye button and run the needle back and forth several times, catching the buttons at each pass and pulling them inward a little each time. When you feel the eyes are securely fastened, tie off the thread.

9. Embroider the nose using a satin stitch and the mouth using a straight stitch. Tie off.

10. To make the collar, cut or tear a strip of fabric 5″ by 43″. Press in half lengthwise. Open out and match up the short ends, right sides together. Stitch, then trim the seam. Press the seam open. Refold on the lengthwise fold line and press, especially at the seam.

11. Using double quilting thread and ½″ stitches, run a hand-gathering stitch around the circle, ¼″ from the raw edges. (Fig. 4) Pull up gathers very tightly and tie off.

12. Stitch the collar to the neck by hand.

13. Fold the handle cover piece of velour right sides together. Pin and stitch the top and long edges, leaving the lower edges open. Trim the seam. Turn right side out and insert the ½″ by 6″ dowel into the fabric tube. Stitch the lower edges closed.

14. Run a hand-gathering stitch around the finial circle. Pull up the gathers, adding a bit of stuffing. Place the finial on the end of the covered rattle handle and pull the gathers in very tightly around the handle, tucking in the raw edges with the point of the needle. Hand stitch the turned-under edge to the fabric-covered handle. Tie off.

15. Make a deep indentation in the bear's head through the holes in the center of the gathered fabric of the collar and the bear's head (the eraser end of a pencil works well for this), then insert the covered handle to check the fit. When the handle can be inserted at least 1¼″, add some tacky glue to the hole and insert the handle. Let dry.

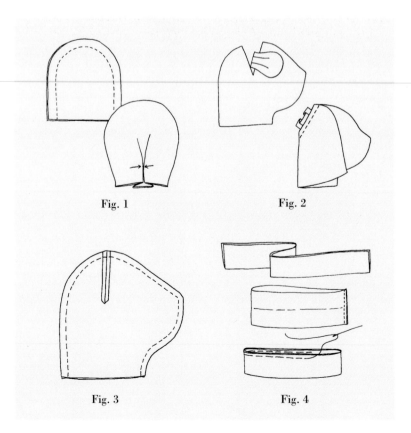

Fig. 1   Fig. 2

Fig. 3   Fig. 4

Bath Time

Hooded Towel

MATERIALS

❖ 1¼ yards of cotton terry velour

❖ ½ yard of cotton fabric to make bias binding or 5 yards of single-fold
  bias tape

❖ ½″ bias tape maker (optional but helpful)

❖ ⅓ yard of white cotton broadcloth

❖ wash-out marking pen or pencil

❖ scraps for appliqués

❖ ¼ yard of fusible web

❖ thread to match bias binding and appliqué fabrics

❖ 12″ by 12″ remnant of thin batting

INSTRUCTIONS

Note: If you would like a different appliqué pattern, try one from the cozy
blankets projects.

1. Cut a 40″ square from the terry velour fabric and round the corners using
    the hood triangle pattern (page 111).

2. Cut several strips of bias 1″ wide and stitch them together end-to-end
    until you have about five yards (180″). Cut one more strip of bias 1″wide
    by 12″long. Fold the long raw edges to meet in the center of the strip,
    pressing as you go, or run it through a ½″ bias tape maker and press.

3. Cut two 12″squares of white cotton broadcloth. Using a wash-out marking
    pen or pencil, mark one square with the hood triangle pattern by tracing.
    (Fig. 1) Mark placement of appliqués and quilting lines as well.

4. Transfer the fish appliqué markings to the paper side of the fusible web by
    tracing. The appliquéd fish will face the opposite direction of the pattern
    pieces but the same direction as indicated on the hood triangle pattern.

5. Cut out each paper-backed fusible web appliqué piece, leaving ¼″ of
    extra space around all the edges.

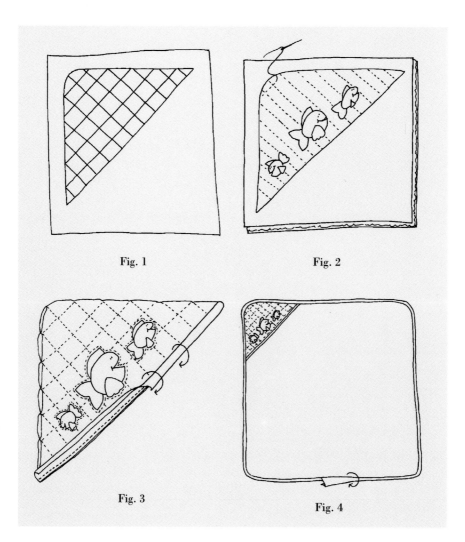

Fig. 1

Fig. 2

Fig. 3

Fig. 4

6. Decide what color you would like each piece to be and fuse the paper-backed web to the wrong side of the corresponding appliqué fabrics. Then, cut out each piece accurately on the lines you traced on the paper side. Peel the paper off each piece and place in its appropriate spot on the marked cotton broadcloth hood triangle. Once all of the pieces are laid out, fuse them in place.

7. Using a machine satin stitch, stitch around each appliqué piece. Press.

8. Layer the plain square of white cotton broadcloth, batting, and appliquéd square of cotton broadcloth. Pin the layers together and hand or machine quilt the layers in a ¾″ grid or other pattern that you like. Quilt around the appliqués as well. (Fig. 2)

9. Remeasure the hood pattern against your appliquéd and quilted fabric. If there is a discrepancy, re-mark the hood piece then cut it out carefully.

10. Use the 12″ strip of bias to bind the long edge of the hood triangle. Open out one folded edge of the bias strip and place it right sides together on the front long edge of the triangle, keeping the raw edges even. Stitch through all layers using a ¼″ seam allowance. Turn the folded edge to the back. Pin and blind stitch in place. (Fig. 3)

11. Place the hood triangle on a corner of the 40″ square of terry velour. Pin in place, then baste.

12. Bind all edges with bias binding as you bound the edge of the hood triangle. (Fig. 4)

Washcloth

MATERIALS

❧ 9″ by 9″ remnant of cotton terry velour fabric

❧ ¼ yard cotton fabric to make binding or 36″ of bias tape

❧ ½″ bias tape maker (optional)

❧ thread to match binding

INSTRUCTIONS

1. Cut an 8″ square of terry velour fabric and round off the corners using the Hooded Towel hood triangle pattern (page 111) as a guide.

2. Cut enough 1″ bias strips to make 36″ of bias binding. Stitch the strips together end to end, if necessary, to make one piece. Fold each long raw edge to the center and press, or run it through a ½″ bias tape maker and press.

3. Pin the binding to the terry velour, right sides together, matching raw edges. Begin pinning the binding at the center of a corner and pin until about 2″ from completing the entire edge. (Fig. 1)

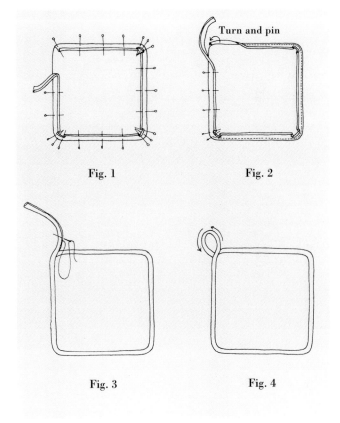

Fig. 1

Turn and pin

Fig. 2

Fig. 3

Fig. 4

4. Stitch a ¼″ seam about halfway around. Turn the folded edge of the first 2″ of binding to the back of the washcloth as if finishing, and pin in place. (Fig. 2) Finish pinning the remaining bias to the edge of the cloth, matching the raw edges and overlapping the beginning raw end by about ¼″, and leaving the extra as a tail. Continue stitching the second half of the binding to finish the edge.

5. Turn the rest of the folded edge of the binding to the back side of the washcloth, pin in place and blind stitch, including the tail, to stitch the layers together. (Fig. 3) Fold the tail to form a loop and fold the raw end under ¼″. Pin to the back side of the washcloth at the bound edge and stitch in place. (Fig. 4)

Covered Sponges

Note: These covered sponges are good bath toys for babies and can be machine-washed. You can also get them wet and chill them in the refrigerator and let a teething baby chew on them. Patterns are on page 112.

MATERIALS

❖ remnants of various colors of terry cloth or cotton velour fabric (or cut the good spots from old towels)
❖ several 2″ thick soft sponges
❖ paper
❖ thread
❖ ¼ yard tear-away stabilizer
❖ fine-point marking pen

INSTRUCTIONS

1. Trace the fabric cutting lines and faces onto the stabilizer with a fine-point marking pen. **Note:** You will need two stabilizer boat shapes to make one boat sponge. Cut out the shapes.
2. Trace the sponge cutting lines onto paper and cut out each shape. Pin the paper pattern on top of the sponge and cut the shape out of the sponge using very sharp scissors.

Sea Star

1. Cut two sea star shapes from terry cloth according to the pattern. Layer the stabilizer sea star on the right side of one fabric sea star and machine satin stitch the eyes and mouth. Tear off the stabilizer and trim the threads.
2. Place both terry cloth sea star shapes right sides together and pin. Stitch a ¼″ seam around all edges, leaving inside "legs" seam open, as indicated on the pattern.
3. Turn right side out and stuff with the cut sponge shape, working it into place. Blind stitch the opening closed.

Fish

1. Cut two of each fish pattern piece from fabric. Layer the stabilizer fish body on the right side of one fabric fish body and machine satin stitch the eyes and mouth. Tear off the stabilizer and trim the threads.
2. Place the two tail sections wrong sides together. Add the layer of stabilizer on top and pin. Stitch around the outer edges of the tail (not the edges that will be in the seam of the fish body) using a ¼″ seam. Then, using a machine satin stitch, go around each piece again using the first row of stitches as the outside edge.
3. Trim close to satin stitches.
4. Satin stitch the lines on tail and remove the stabilizer.
5. Repeat steps 2 through 4 for fin and flippers.

6. Place the fin and tail on the fish body at the placement lines, matching the raw edges. Stitch in place.

7. Place the second fish body section right sides together on the first fish body section. Using a ¼″ seam, sew the body sections together leaving a 2″ opening on the bottom edge. Turn right side out.

8. Stuff with precut sponge and blind stitch the opening closed.

9. Stitch the flippers to the sides at placement lines.

Boat

1. Cut two 6″ by 6″ pieces of white terry cloth and cut two boat shapes (without the sails) from blue terry cloth using the pattern. (Fig. 1)

2. Place one blue boat on each white terry cloth square. Layer one stabilizer boat on each and pin.

3. Machine satin stitch from the X's at the top of the mast to the boat and across the top of the boat. (Fig. 2) Remove the stabilizer.

4. Place the pattern on the blue and white pieces one at a time and cut on the outermost line. Trim away the white fabric from the back of the pieces ¼″ above the top satin stitching and ¼″ below the bottom satin stitching. This will remove the bulk of the extra layers.

5. Pin the boat pieces right sides together and stitch a ¼″ seam, leaving one sail seam open. Turn right side out.

6. Stuff with the precut sponge shape and blind stitch the opening closed.

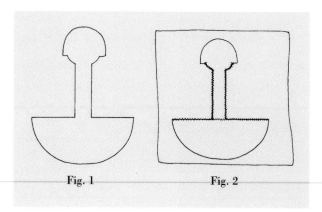

Fig. 1   Fig. 2

Wall Organizer

This is a great help for keeping bath time supplies organized and handy. The mesh pockets allow a place for wet bath toys to dry out when bathing is done.

MATERIALS

❖ ⅝ yard of white cotton terry velour
❖ 10″ by 14″ remnant of white cotton broadcloth
❖ ¼ yard of mesh fabric (not netting)
❖ scraps for appliqués
❖ ¼ yard of binding fabric or 3½ yards of bias tape
❖ ½″ bias tape maker (optional)
❖ wash-out marking pen
❖ ¼ yard of tear-away stabilizer
❖ 1 yard of ¼″ elastic
❖ 12″ wide child-size hanger
❖ thread (colors to match appliqué and binding fabrics)
❖ black embroidery floss

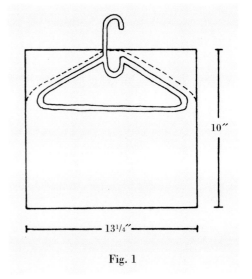

Fig. 1

INSTRUCTIONS

1. Cut a rectangle of white cotton broadcloth 13¼″ wide by 10″ long.
2. Cut a rectangle of white terry velour fabric that measures 13¼″ wide by 26″ long.
3. Lay the hanger on the cotton broadcloth so the top arch of the shoulder curve is ⅝″ below the upper raw edge. Trace the shoulder curve of the hanger, leaving a ⅝″ space between the hanger and the line you are drawing. (Fig. 1) The tracing should end at the left and right side raw edges of the fabric.
4. Lay the cotton broadcloth with the tracing marked on it on the rectangle of terry velour, catching the upper raw edges. Pin and cut both fabrics on the traced line. **Note:** The terry velour piece will be called "organizer" and the cotton broadcloth piece will be called "sleeve" in the instructions that follow.
5. For the top pocket, cut one piece of terry velour 6″ wide by 5½″ long.
6. For triple center pockets, cut one piece of terry velour 22¼″ wide by 6½″ long.
7. For bottom pockets, cut one piece of mesh fabric 14¼″ wide by 7½″ long.
8. Cut enough 1″ wide bias strips to make 3½ yards of binding. Using ¼″ seams, stitch the strips end-to-end to make one long strip. Press the seams in one direction. Fold the long raw edges to the center and press or run it through a ½″ bias tape maker and press.
9. To bind the top edge of each pocket piece, place the binding on the fabric, right sides together, matching the raw edges. Stitch a ¼″ seam. Turn the folded edge of the binding to the back side of the pocket piece; pin and blind stitch in place.
10. Cut the fish, sea star, and octopus appliqués (page 113) out of the fabric scraps. Place each on its respective pocket and sandwich it between two layers of stabilizer. Pin all the layers together well. Machine satin stitch around each appliqué piece and each smile using the appropriate color thread. Straight stitch the fish flipper and tail details.

11. Tear the stabilizer off both sides and trim the threads.

12. Use four strands of embroidery floss to make French knot eyes.

13. Thread a 20″ piece of elastic through the binding of the center triple pocket and a 16″ piece through the binding of the mesh pockets.

14. Use the following diagrams to guide you in folding the tucks and placing the pockets.

15. Mark the center line of the bottom mesh pocket and organizer pieces. Pin the mesh pocket to the organizer matching side raw edges. Stitch a ¼″ seam. Match the center lines and pin. Satin stitch the pockets to the organizer on the center line. To take up the extra fabric at the bottom edge, make ½″ tucks at each side of each pocket (four tucks in all; Fig. 2). Pin the tucked lower edge of the pockets to the lower raw edge of the organizer and stitch a ¼″ seam. Keep the folds of the tucks ⅛″ from the side seams so they won't get caught in the binding process.

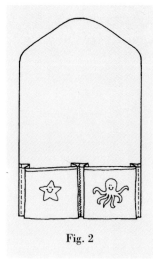

Fig. 2

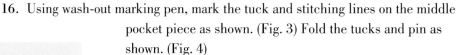

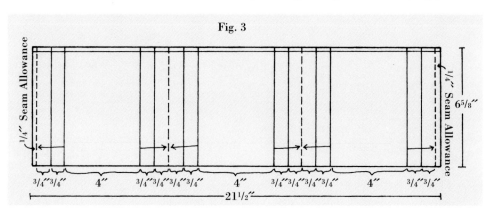

Fig. 3

¼″ Seam Allowance

¼″ Seam Allowance

6⅝″

3/4″ 3/4″   4″   3/4″ 3/4″ 3/4″ 3/4″   4″   3/4″ 3/4″ 3/4″ 3/4″   4″   3/4″ 3/4″

21½″

16. Using wash-out marking pen, mark the tuck and stitching lines on the middle pocket piece as shown. (Fig. 3) Fold the tucks and pin as shown. (Fig. 4)

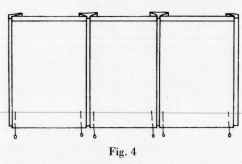

Fig. 4

17. Lay the tucked fabric on the organizer facedown so the unbound bottom edge is 10″ from the bottom of the organizer (Fig. 5; it is upside down at this point). Pin and stitch a ½″ seam across the bottom edge of the pockets. (Fig. 5) Flip the pocket up and pin the sides, matching the raw edges, and stitch ¼″ seams. Pin the stitching lines that will separate the pockets to the organizer, making sure they are straight and evenly spaced, and topstitch in place.

18. Fold the side raw edges of the top pocket under ½″ and press. Place the pocket on the organizer facedown so the unbound bottom edge is 2½″ above the top of the center pockets (it is upside down at this point). Center it left to right as well. Pin and stitch a ½″ seam across the bottom of the pocket. Flip the pocket up and pin the folded side edges to the organizer and topstitch in place.

19. To hem the bottom edge of the sleeve, turn the lower edge (opposite the shoulder curve) under ¼″ and press. Turn under ¼″ again and press. Topstitch in place.

20. Double fold the top center of the shoulder curve (¼″ twice) and topstitch. This makes room for the hook of the hanger to come through.

21. Pin the sleeve to the back of the organizer and stitch a ¼″ seam around the sides and top edges, making sure the hole for the hanger is open.

22. Bind the outer edges in the same manner as you bound the pocket edges.

23. Insert the hanger.

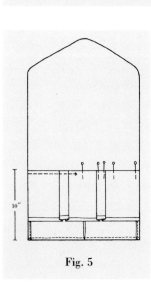

10″

Fig. 5

Christening Gown

MATERIALS

- ❖ 2 yards of fine cotton batiste
- ❖ 3 yards of ½" French lace insertion
- ❖ 4 yards of Swiss embroidered insertion with entredeux edges
- ❖ 4 yards of 1½" French lace edging
- ❖ 1 yard of French lace beading
- ❖ 1¼ yards of ¼" wide satin ribbon
- ❖ 2 pearl buttons
- ❖ 60-weight thread (also called lingerie thread)
- ❖ spray starch
- ❖ very fine glass head pins (not plastic, they will melt under the heat of the iron)
- ❖ size 70/10 machine needles
- ❖ wash-out marking pen or pencil
- ❖ open-toe embroidery foot for your sewing machine

INSTRUCTIONS

It is very important in French sewing projects like this that all the pieces be on the grain of the fabric. Most of the pieces are straight-edged so it makes cutting them quite simple. To maintain the fabric grain down the length of a strip of fabric, you must pull a thread of the fabric and then cut on the line left by the absent thread. To begin, make a small snip into the edge of the fabric and then grasp one thread from either side of the snip. Pull it carefully but firmly, coaxing the fabric to move along the thread. If the thread breaks (and it probably will as these threads are quite fine), cut along the line as far as it goes and pick up another thread and continue. Sometimes, when you are pulling threads to mark the fold lines for making tucks in the fabric, the thread will break and you cannot cut into the fabric to retrieve the thread. You will need to find the broken end of the thread and pull it out about an inch above the break with the point of a pin. As you practice the thread pulling technique, it will become easier.

Note: Cut out all pieces according to the layout diagram and patterns given on pages 66 and 114–115.

In sewing this garment, you will use a few techniques that are described below. You can refer to these instructions as needed in the construction process. There are spaces provided for you to write down the machine length and width settings that work best for you, so you can adjust your sewing machine easily each time.

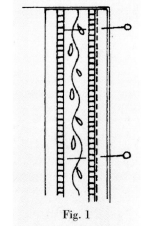

Fig. 1

Technique A, Entredeux to flat fabric:
The words *entredeux* and *insertion* are used interchangeably here because the Swiss insertion used has an entredeux edge.

1. Cut the required length of Swiss embroidered insertion. The Swiss insertions come with a ¼" seam allowance on each side. Matching the raw edges, pin the insertion to the fabric, right sides together. Straight stitch as close as

Christening Gown Fabric Layout Diagram

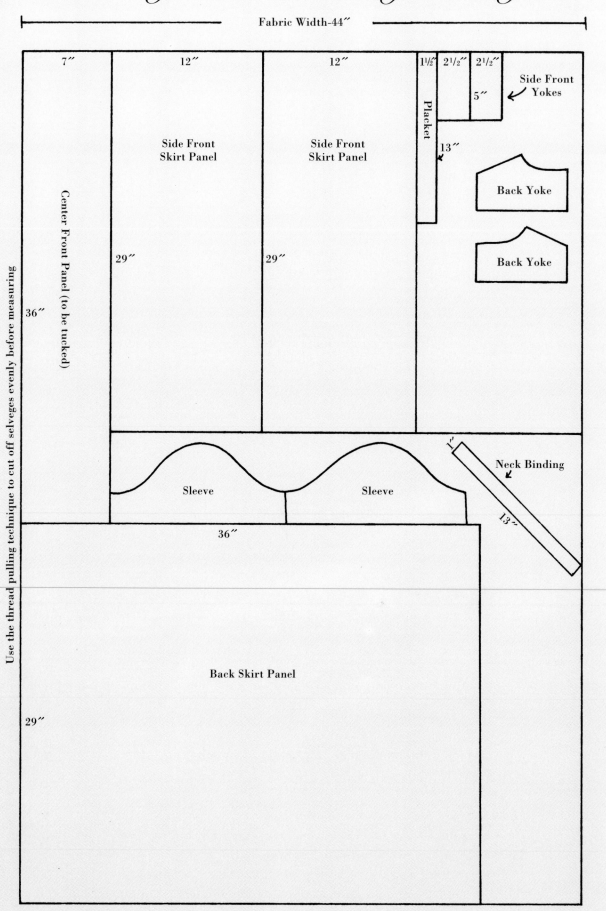

Fabric Width-44"

Use the thread pulling technique to cut off selveges evenly before measuring

Center Front Panel (to be tucked)

7"

36"

Side Front
Skirt Panel

12"

29"

Side Front
Skirt Panel

12"

29"

Placket

1½" 2½" 2½"

5"

Side Front
Yokes

13"

Back Yoke

Back Yoke

Sleeve

Sleeve

36"

Neck Binding

1"

13"

Back Skirt Panel

29"

possible to the entredeux edge of the insertion. (Fig. 1) An open-toe embroidery foot on your sewing machine is very helpful in making it easier to see your stitching line as you go.

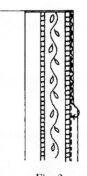

2. Trim the raw edges of the fabric and insertion ⅛″. Now stitch again, using a zigzag stitch in which the left swing of the needle goes into the previous line of stitches and the right swing of the needle goes off the edge of the fabric. The zigzag will roll the raw edge over and encase it in thread. (Fig. 2) Press the Swiss insertions outward. You will need to take a few minutes to fine-tune the length and width settings on your sewing machine to do this, but they should be somewhere around length: 1, width: 3½. Once you find the settings, the stitching process goes very quickly.

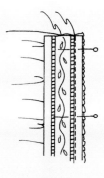

Fig. 2

3. My settings: length_____ width_____

Technique B, Entredeux to gathered fabric

1. Run two rows of gathering stitches along the edge to be gathered, ⅛″ and ⅜″ from the raw edge. Pull up the bobbin threads to gather the fabric to fit the required length of the Swiss insertion. Pin the gathered edge to the Swiss insertion, adjusting the gathers evenly.

2. Straight stitch as close as possible to the entredeux edge of the insertion. (Fig. 3)

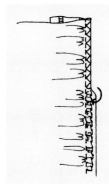

Fig. 3

3. Trim the gathered fabric seam allowance to ⅟₁₆″ and the insertion seam allowance to ⅛″. Turn over and stitch again from the opposite side, using a zigzag stitch in which the left swing of the needle goes into the previous line of stitches and the right swing of the needle goes off the edge of the fabric. The zigzag will roll the raw edge of the insertion over the gathered raw edge and encase it in thread. (Fig. 4)

4. My settings: length_____width_____

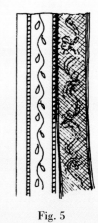

Fig. 4

Technique C, Flat lace to entredeux

1. Carefully trim the fabric seam allowance off one edge of the required length of entredeux.

2. Lightly spray starch and press the entredeux and lace.

3. With right sides up, butt the trimmed edge of the entredeux to the edge of the lace under the presser foot of your sewing machine (do not overlap them—see Fig. 5). Zigzag stitch them together, carefully feeding them through the machine side by side. The needle should swing wide enough to enter the holes of the entredeux on one side and catch the heading of the lace on the other. Again, you will need to take a few minutes to adjust the length and width of the machine to make the best stitches for the task. Try a length of 2 and a width of 2½, and adjust from there. If you are a perfectionist, it is possible to adjust your settings so the needle will go into each hole of the entredeux.

4. My settings: length_____ width_____

Technique D, Gathered lace edging to entredeux

1. Cut the required length of French lace edging. The heading (top flat edge) of the French lace edging has a few threads running through it that you can pull to gather the lace. Use the point of a pin to extract the

Fig. 5

end of one of the heading threads and pull to gather the lace to fit the edge to which it will be attached.

2 Carefully trim the fabric seam allowance off one edge of the required length of entredeux.

3. With right sides up, butt the trimmed edge of the entredeux to the gathered edge of the lace (do not overlap them), under the presser foot of your sewing machine. Zigzag stitch them together, carefully feeding them through the machine side by side. The gathered lace will need to be coaxed under the presser foot with the point of a seam ripper or bamboo skewer, so it doesn't lose its gathers in the process. The needle should swing wide enough to enter the holes of the entredeux on one side and catch the heading of the lace on the other. These length and width settings should be the same as for technique C, but you should still do a trial run.

4. My settings: length_____ width_____

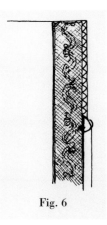

Fig. 6

Technique E, Flat lace to fabric

1. Lightly spray starch the lace and press. Press the fabric also.
2. With right sides together, lay the lace on the fabric ⅛″ from the raw edge.
3. Stitch the lace to the fabric using a zigzag stitch. (Fig. 6) The left swing of the needle should go into the lace heading and the right swing of the needle should go off the edge of the fabric to roll the raw edge over and encase the edge in thread. For settings, try a length of ½ and a width of 4, and adjust from there to make a nicely finished edge. The rolled seam will want to be pressed toward the lace.
4. My settings: length_____ width_____

Gown Center Panel

1. On the center front panel strip (7″ wide by 36″ long), mark the tuck folding lines by pulling the lengthwise threads as shown. (Fig. 7)

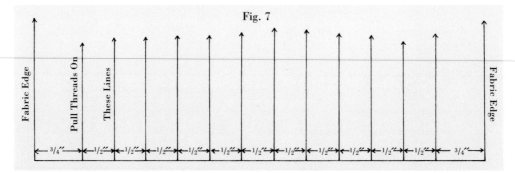

Fig. 7

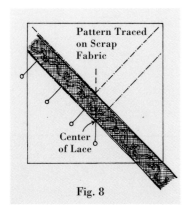

Pattern Traced on Scrap Fabric

Center of Lace

Fig. 8

2. When all the threads are pulled, you can begin to make the tucks in the fabric. Fold the fabric exactly on the first pulled thread line. Stitch an accurate ⅛″ from the folded edge. Press the folded edge toward the nearest raw edge. Continue folding, stitching, and pressing the tucks until all 12 tucks are done. Six should be pressed to the right and six to the left.

3. Transfer the pattern given for the lace "V" (page 114) shape to a scrap of muslin or other cloth. Place the cloth scrap with the pattern tracing smoothly on the ironing board.

4. Cut five 7″ pieces of ½″ wide French insertion lace. Pin one of these lace strips on the "V"-shape pattern, having the center

point of the lower lace heading match the lower center point of the "V." Anchor the heading of the lace with pins through the pattern and into the ironing board cover at the bottom center point and along the lower edges of the left-hand side of the "V" shape. (Fig. 8) **Note:** When pinning the lace to the ironing board cover, place the pins at as much of a horizontal angle as possible because you will be ironing on the pins later.

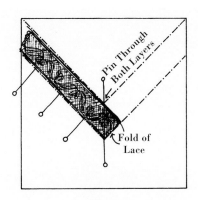

Fig. 9

5. Fold the other half of the lace back on the pinned half, matching the headings exactly. Place a pin through both layers of lace at the inside point of the "V" shape (Fig. 9). Now fold the top layer back to lie on the right-hand side of the "V" shape. (Fig. 10) Pin the remaining edges of the lace to the pattern and ironing board. You should have a nicely mitered corner.

6. Lightly spray starch the lace "V" shape and press. Gently remove the lace and use a tiny zigzag stitch to stitch the mitered corner. Repeat for all five lace "V" shapes.

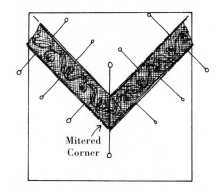

Fig. 10

7. Lay the first lace "V" shape on the tucked panel of fabric, with the point of the "V" being centered 7″ down from the upper raw edge of the fabric. Make sure the left and right sides are evenly spaced from the top edge as well (they should be a bit wider than the tucked panel, which will be trimmed later). Hand-baste in place, then use a tiny zigzag stitch onto the tucked panel. Repeat for all five lace "V" shapes leaving 6″ between the bottom point of one and the bottom point of the next one. (Fig. 11)

8. *Carefully* trim the fabric away from behind the lace "V" shapes. I use round-end scissors called "pocket" scissors for this job. They look like kindergarten scissors, but the blades are very sharp. Trim the extra lace from the edges as well so the sides of the panel are straight.

9. Cut two 36″ lengths of ⅜″-wide Swiss embroidered insertion. Pin one to each side of the tucked panel,

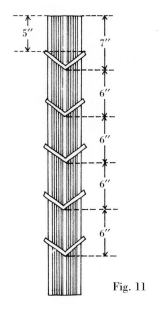

Fig. 11

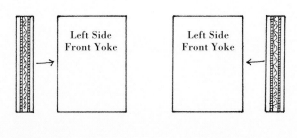

Fig. 12

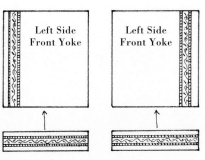

Fig. 13

69

right sides together, matching the raw edges. Using technique A, stitch the entredeux edge of the insertion to the tucked panel. Press the Swiss insertions outward. Set this center panel aside.

Fig. 14

Fig. 15

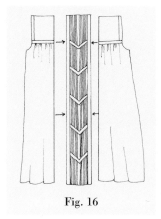

Fig. 16

Gown Front Side Panels

1. Using technique A, stitch a strip of Swiss embroidered insertion to the sleeve edge of each side front yoke piece (Fig. 12) and another strip across the bottom edge of each piece. (Fig. 13)
2. Lay the side front skirt panels (12″ wide by 29″ long) right sides together and trace the underarm curve onto the top piece, matching the top and side edges. (Fig. 14) Cut the underarm curve on both layers.
3. Using technique B, sew the side front skirt panels to the side front yokes. (Fig. 15)

Gown Front

1. To attach the side panels to the center panel, place the left-side panel right sides together with the center panel, having the horizontal strip of Swiss embroidered insertion meet the uppermost lace "V" shape at the edge. (Fig. 16) Use technique A to stitch the panels together. Repeat for the right side panel.
2. Press the front panel.

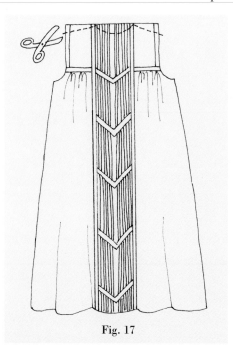

Fig. 17

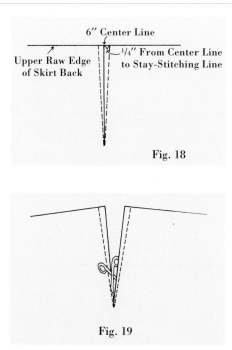

6″ Center Line

Upper Raw Edge
of Skirt Back

¼″ From Center Line
to Stay-Stitching Line

Fig. 18

Fig. 19

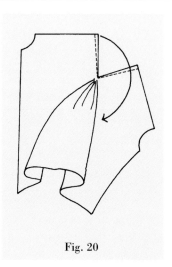

Fig. 20

3. Lay the front yoke pattern across the top of the front panel, matching side edges and centers. Using wash-out marking pen or pencil, trace the yoke pattern onto the front panel fabric. Cut away the extra fabric at shoulders and neck to leave a front panel with yoke. (Fig. 17) Set aside.

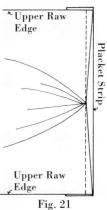

Fig. 21

Gown Back

1. Transfer the underarm curve to each corner of the back skirt panel (36″ wide by 29″ long), matching the side and upper raw edges. Cut away the fabric to make the underarm curves.
2. Find the center of the upper edge of the back skirt panel by folding. Mark a 6″ line from the raw edge down and mark a stay-stitching line as shown. (Fig. 18) Use a small machine stitch and stitch on the stay-stitching line. Carefully cut on the center line to the pivot point of the stay-stitching. (Fig. 19)
3. Pull the slit fabric open (Fig. 20) to make a wide "V" shape. The stay-stitching line should be in a straight line.
4. Lay the placket strip right sides together with the slit in the back skirt panel (the placket strip being the bottom layer). The stay-stitching line should be parallel to the long raw edge of the placket strip. (Fig. 21) Pin in place and stitch through both layers on the stay-stitching line, being careful not to catch any extra fabric at the pivot point.
5. Press the seam toward the placket strip.
6. Turn the long raw edge of the placket strip under ¼″ and press. Turn this folded edge to the inside, just to the stitching line. (Fig. 22) Pin and blind stitch in place.
7. Run a diagonal row of stitches across the bottom fold of the placket. (Fig. 23)
8. Turn the left side of the placket to the inside and baste across the top edge.
9. Fold the back yoke plackets to the inside on the fold lines as the pattern indicates and press. (Fig. 24)
10. Run two rows of machine gathering stitches along the upper raw edges of the back skirt panel (on both sides of the placket) ⅛″ and ⅜″ from the raw edge.
11. Pin the back yokes to the upper raw edges of the back skirt panel, right sides together, pulling up the bobbin threads to gather the skirt edges. Match raw edges and sleeve edge corners. The skirt placket should meet the fold line of the yoke facings. Fold the yoke facings around to the

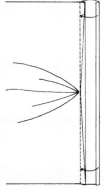

Fig. 22

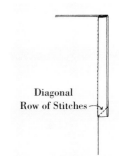

Diagonal Row of Stitches

Fig. 23

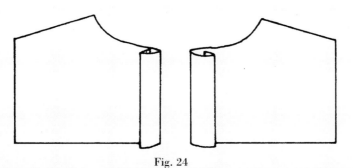

Fig. 24

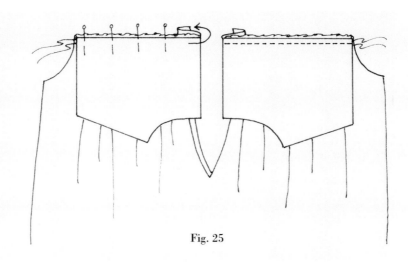

Fig. 25

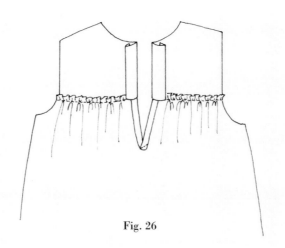

Fig. 26

wrong side of the gathered skirt and pin. (Fig. 25) Stitch a ¼″ seam. Trim
the seam allowances to ⅛″ and zigzag satin stitch the raw edges.

12. Fold the back yokes upward and the facings will automatically fold them-
selves to the inside. (Fig. 26) Press.

Assembling the Gown

1. Pin the gown front to the gown back at the shoulders, *wrong* sides together. Stitch ¼″ seams at the shoulders. Trim the seam allowances to ⅛″ and
press the seams toward the back. Then fold the gown at the shoulder
seams so it is right sides together. Pin and stitch another ¼″ seam. This
method, called French seaming, encloses the raw edge of the seam, which
makes it look better and last longer because the threads of the seam
allowances cannot unravel.

2. Stay-stitch the neck edge by straight stitching ¼″ from the raw edge.

3. Fold one long raw edge of the bias neck binding to the center and press.
Press the bias into a curved shape having the raw edge be the inside of
the curve.

4. Pin the bias neck binding to the neck of the gown, matching the curved
raw edges and leaving ½″ tails at each end. Carefully stitch a ¼″ seam.

5. Turn under the ½″ tails and turn the folded edge of the binding to the
inside of the neck and pin. Blind stitch in place.

6. Using French seams, stitch the side seams of the gown.

7. Trim the lower edge of the gown so it is even all around.

8. Cut a 68″ length each of ½″ French insertion lace and Swiss embroidered insertion. Cut a 102″ length of 1½″ French lace edging.

9. Using technique C, stitch the French lace and Swiss insertions together.

10. Using technique D, gather the lace edging and stitch it to the Swiss insertion.

11. Using technique E, stitch the lace band to the lower edge of the gown, leaving 1″ extra at each end. Then French seam the raw ends of the lace bands.

12. Cut two 15″ lengths of lace beading and two 23″ lengths of 1½″ French lace edging for the sleeves.

13. Use technique D to gather and stitch the lace edging to the beading (you will be catching the heading of the beading instead of the entredeux holes). Repeat to make two pieces.

14. Use technique E to sew the beading to the lower edge of each sleeve.

15. Beginning and ending at the ♥'s, as indicated on the pattern, run two rows of gathering threads around the cap of each sleeve, ⅛″ and ⅜″ from the raw edge.

16. French seam the underarm seam of each sleeve. (Fig. 27)

17. Pin the sleeve, right sides together, to the gown, matching the top center of the sleeve to the shoulder seam and matching the underarm seams. Pull up the bobbin threads and adjust the sleeve gathers evenly.

18. Stitch a ¼″ seam. Part of the seam sleeve will be sewn to the entredeux edge of the front yoke, so be sure to stitch as close as possible to the entredeux edge.

19. Trim the seam allowances to ⅛″ and zigzag satin stitch the raw edges.

20. Thread a 20″ length of ¼″ satin ribbon through the beading holes.

21. Mark the buttonholes on the left-hand back yoke (the one that is on top when the plackets are overlapped) and stitch by hand or machine.

22. Mark the button placement and sew the buttons on the right-hand back yoke.

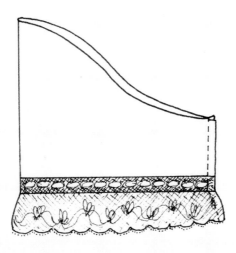

Fig. 27

73

Carriage Blanket and Pillow

MATERIALS

❧ 1½ yards very soft wool flannel

❧ 1½ yards flannel-backed satin (sometimes called Cuddleskin™)

❧ scraps of camel-colored wool flannel for the bear appliqués

❧ 3 yards of 2″ wide cotton lace trim (crochet, tatted, or cluny)

❧ thread to match the blanket and appliqué fabric

❧ #5 perle cotton in DMC colors 225, 415, 503, 504, 746, 762, 3042

❧ 1¾″ pearl button

❧ dark brown embroidery floss

❧ wash-out marking pen

❧ ⅜ yard cotton broadcloth or ticking

❧ stuffing or feathers (you can recycle an old pillow for this)

INSTRUCTIONS

Note: Patterns are on page 116.

1. Cut a 36″ by 36″ square of the wool fabric. Cut a 36″ by 38″ piece of the flannel-backed satin.

2. Using the wash-out marking pen, transfer the bear design to the 36″ square wool fabric, 9″ down from the upper raw edge and centered left to right.

3. Transfer the bear pattern pieces to the right side of the camel-colored wool flannel. Using a tiny machine stitch and matching thread, stay-stitch around each piece.

4. Cut out each piece leaving a generous ⅛″ seam allowance. Clip the curved edges to the stay-stitching line.

5. Each bear piece is labeled with a number. Appliqué the pieces to the blanket in numerical order. Pin the first piece to the blanket on its corresponding spot and stitch in place using a blind stitch, turning the edges under with the point of the needle as you go. The stay-stitching line on the appliqué fabric will match the marking pen line on the blanket to help you keep the pieces in the proper places as you stitch. You do not need to turn under the edges that will be covered by another piece. Simply tack them down with a small running stitch. Stitch all the bear pieces in place in the same manner.

6. Use one strand of dark brown floss to embroider the bears' faces as indicated on the pattern. Use French knots for the eyes, padded satin stitch for the nose, and stem stitch for the mouth. Work the flowers using perle cotton and a lazy daisy stitch for the petals and leaves and French knots for the centers.

7. Cut a 36″ length of lace and pin it across the blanket front 1½″ below the upper raw edge. Topstitch in place. (Fig. 1)

8. Place the wool blanket right sides together with the flannel-backed satin,

matching the side and lower edges. Stitch a ¼″ seam on all three sides. Clip corners and turn right side out. Press so the edges are crisply turned out.

9. Fold the upper side edges of the satin in ¼″ and press. (Fig. 2) Fold the raw edge of the flannel-backed satin ½″ to the inside and press. Fold again to make a 1½″ binding across the top of the blanket. (Fig. 3) The fold should just overlap the edge of the lace by ⅛″. Pin and blind stitch in place.

10. Choose a color of perle cotton and stitch a running stitch, or other decorative stitch, around the side and bottom edges of the blanket about 1½″ in from the edge.

Pillow

1. Cut one 12½″ by 16½″ piece of wool fabric for the pillow front. Cut two 12½″ by 11½″ pieces for the pillow backs.

2. Using the lazy daisy stitch and French knots, embroider some flowers scattered around the pillow top.

3. To form the button placket on the center of each back section, fold under ¼″ on each back on the first fold line and press. Fold each again 2″ in on the second fold line and press. Edge-stitch or blind stitch the placket in place along the folded edge. (Fig. 4)

4. Stitch a ⅞″ buttonhole on the center of one back placket.

5. With both right sides up, overlap the plackets, having the one with the buttonhole on top. Make sure the left and right side raw edges measure 16½″ between them (Fig. 5) and adjust if necessary. Pin the edges of the plackets together and baste.

6. Lay the front right sides together with the backs, matching the raw edges and corners. Pin and stitch around the perimeter using a ¼″ seam.

7. Clip the corners and turn right side out.

8. Sew the button on the under placket to correspond with the buttonhole.

9. Whipstitch the lace edging around the edges of the pillow cover.
Note: If you are using an eyelet lace edging, you will need to baste it in place before sewing the front to the back so the raw edge will be in the seam.

10. To make the pillow insert, cut two 12″ by 16″ pieces of cotton fabric and place them right sides together. Stitch around the edges using a ¼″ seam and leaving a 3″ opening in one side for turning. Turn right side out and stuff lightly with stuffing or feathers through the opening. Turn the raw edges to the inside and pin. Blind stitch the opening closed. Insert the pillow into the pillow cover.

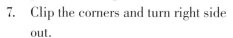

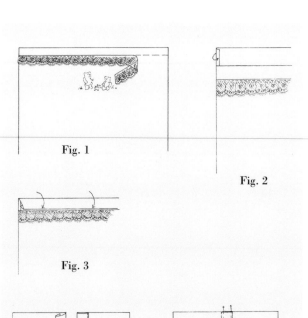

Fig. 1

Fig. 2

Fig. 3

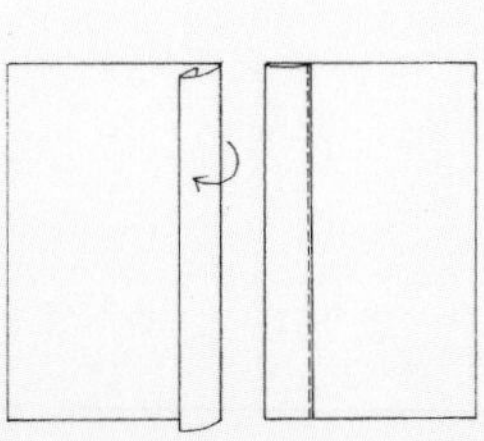

Fig. 4

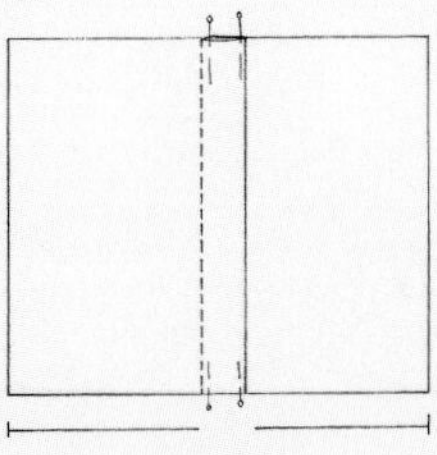

16½″

Fig. 5

Antique Handkerchiefs

Antique handkerchiefs are very beautiful and fairly easy to find. You may even have a few special ones tucked away somewhere waiting to be used and enjoyed, but you're afraid of harming them. A wonderful way to display these treasures is to embroider a record of your baby's or grandbaby's birth on one and have it framed. It will be a special heirloom to cherish now and to pass on to your children's children. If you don't have any beautiful handkerchiefs in your possession, you can usually acquire them reasonably at antiques shops, vintage clothing and textile shows, or flea markets. Even the search is fun. The great part about this project is that most of the work is already done for you. In a matter of hours, you can create a very special gift for a very special person in your life.

Sometimes you will find a handkerchief that is damaged in some way, but you love it anyway. It can still be used. If the center fabric has holes in it, you can do the embroidery on a different piece of fabric (usually a piece of similar vintage fabric as it has a mellowed appearance to it) and replace the damaged section in the mounting and framing process. A fragile bit of lace border can be repaired and when framed will be subjected only to admiration, not wear and tear.

Karen Elizabeth Layman

October 8, 1993

Handkerchief Birth Record

MATERIALS

❧ antique handkerchief

❧ wash-out fine-tip pencil or marking pen

❧ embroidery floss (colors as desired)

INSTRUCTIONS

1. Gently wash the handkerchief. To dry the handkerchief, roll it in a soft towel to remove as much water as you can. Never wring out an antique textile. Then place it facedown on a soft towel on the ironing board and press it dry on a low setting. Sometimes lace edges need to be blocked to dry. In this case, using very fine pins, pin the lace edges to the ironing board about every ¼″ or as often as needed to restore the shape of the lace. If you use glass head pins, you can press the handkerchief dry.

2. Transfer the embroidery design on page 117 to the handkerchief by tracing, using a wash-out fine-tip pencil or marker.

3. Work the embroidery design according to the pattern, referring to the Stitch Reference (page 126) for help with making the stitches.

4. When the embroidery is done, wash the handkerchief again to remove any oil left by your hands as it will eventually discolor the work if left in. Press the damp handkerchief facedown on a soft towel until dry.

5. Frame as desired.

Antique Handkerchief Picture

Note: All the stitches were worked using one strand of floss and a #10 crewel needle. See the Stitch Reference for help with the stitches. All floss color numbers given are DMC. Patterns are on page 117.

Padded satin stitch

inside bear's ears   DMC 840

bear's paws   DMC 840

bear's bow   DMC 304

bear's nose   DMC 310

Annie's nose   DMC 304

Bullion stitch

Annie's hair   DMC 3721 and DMC 3722 (do some stitches in each color)

Shadow work stitch

Annie's face and arms   ecru

Annie's dress   DMC 3747

Annie's collar and petticoats   white

Annie's shoe   DMC 310

Annie's stocking stripes   DMC 304

French knots

Note: The lines on the pattern that separate the light brown from the dark brown are for guidance only; the actual knots were intermingled around the line location.

bear's light fur   DMC 841

bear's dark fur   DMC 840

bear's eyes   DMC 310

flowers on Annie's dress   DMC 3354

Lazy daisy stitch

leaves on Annie's dress DMC 955

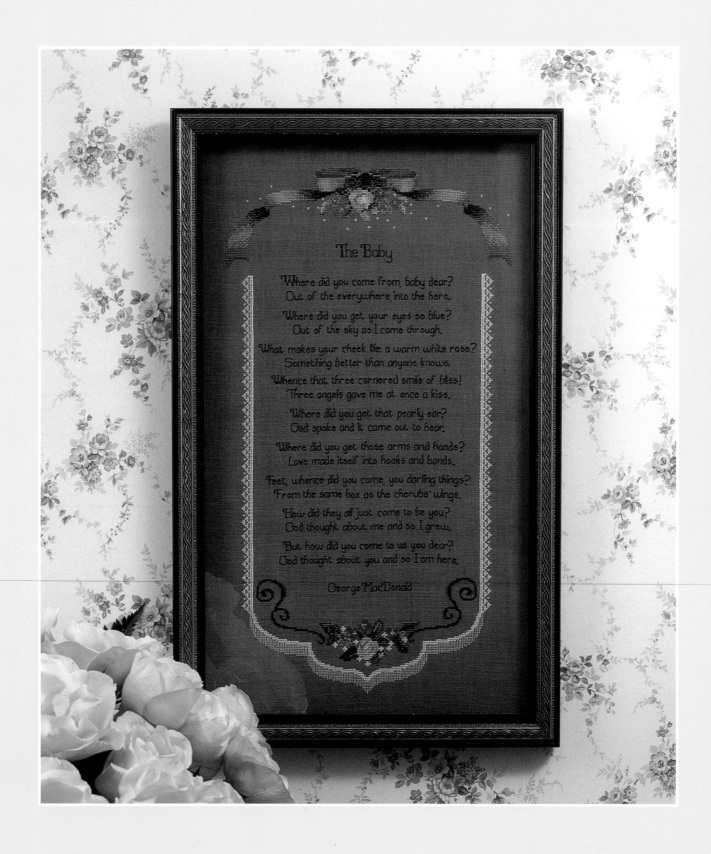

The Baby

Where did you come from, baby dear?
Out of the everywhere into the here.

Where did you get your eyes so blue?
Out of the sky as I came through.

What makes your cheek like a warm white rose?
Something better than anyone knows.

Whence that three cornered smile of bliss!
Three angels gave me at once a kiss.

Where did you get that pearly ear?
God spoke and it came out to hear.

Where did you get those arms and hands?
Love made itself into hooks and bands.

Feet, whence did you come, you darling things?
From the same box as the cherubs' wings.

How did they all just come to be you?
God thought about me and so I grew.

But how did you come to us you dear?
God thought about you and so I am here.

George MacDonald

"The Baby"
Counted Cross-Stitch

I found this verse in a wonderful book on sewing for infants and immediately wanted to work it on cloth. It is such a delightful account of how babies come to be. With a little research, I discovered it came from a magazine from the early 1900s. I thank the author, George MacDonald, for such sweet poetry.

Counted cross-stitch is a very easy form of needlework to learn. You work on an evenweave fabric like Aida cloth, which is made especially for this work, or linen, which has a more refined look. If you are just beginning at counted cross-stitch, the Aida cloth is a bit easier to work on because every stitch is very well defined by the weave of the fabric. When working on linen, you form the stitches over two threads vertically and horizontally and must be more careful with your stitch placement as each stitch depends on all the other stitches being in just the right place.

MATERIALS
❧ 20″ by 28″ piece of 32-count linen (I used "Barnwood")
   or 16-count Aida cloth
❧ #26 tapestry needle
❧ embroidery hoop
❧ DMC embroidery floss according to the chart (page 82)

INSTRUCTIONS
1. To prepare the fabric, fold in half to find the vertical center and refold to find the horizontal center. Hand-baste a marker thread (contrasting color) that exactly follows the center thread in each direction. This will help in centering the work on the fabric.
2. Zigzag stitch the edges of the fabric to keep it from fraying or treat with a fray-stopping liquid.
3. Cut your floss into lengths that you are comfortable working with. I like mine to be about 24″ long. Separate all six strands and then recombine the number of strands needed. In this case the entire design is worked in two strands of floss over two threads on linen.
4. Each square on the chart represents one stitch on the cloth and the symbol in the square represents the color of the floss to use. So choose a spot, usually very near the center, and thread your needle with the color indicated.

5. Counted cross-stitch requires that no knots be used to start and end the threads because they can interrupt the smooth surface of the finished work. So to begin a thread, push the needle up from the back side of the fabric and pull through until a tail about 1″ long remains on the back. Hold this loose end with your finger by pressing it against the cloth until you can secure it with the first few stitches. End the thread by running the needle through the back of several stitches and cutting the thread close.

6. For horizontal rows of stitches, work half stitches to the end of the row and finish the stitches by working back to the beginning. (Fig. 1)

7. Backstitches are used for forming letters and outlining parts of the design. (Fig. 2)

Note: The chart begins on page 118.

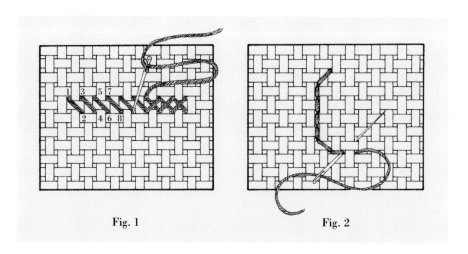

Fig. 1   Fig. 2

Symbol	DMC Color Number	Color Description
-	white	white
O	ecru	ecru
X	3078	golden yellow, very light
2	3021	brown gray, very dark
K	319	pistachio green, very dark
>	320	pistachio green, dark
Z	367	pistachio green, medium
B	368	pistachio green, light
=	369	pistachio green, very light
*	223	shell pink, medium
Q	224	shell pink, light
(	225	shell pink, very light
3	3042	dusty violet, light
7	3041	dusty violet, medium
G	924	teal blue, very dark
V	3768	teal blue, dark
©	926	teal blue, medium
¼	927	teal blue, light
□	928	teal blue, very light

Stitch count—171 stitches wide by 303 stitches high

Finished size—12½″ by 20½″ on 16-count cloth

Picture Frame

This sweet picture frame will accommodate a 4″ by 6″ picture. If you want another design to paint, you can use the design from the lampshade and reduce it to fit on a photocopier.

MATERIALS

❖ 15″ by 22″ sheet of mat or illustration board
❖ X-acto® or craft knife
❖ metal-edge ruler
❖ pencil
❖ tacky glue
❖ ⅜ yard of white cotton fabric
❖ 8″ by 11″ remnant of batting
❖ fabric paints: white, red, and yellow
❖ small paintbrush
❖ brown fine-point permanent fabric marking pen
❖ black fine-point permanent fabric marking pen
❖ 1½ yards of piping
❖ 3 paper brads
Look for the following items in a picture framing store:
❖ 3 turn buttons (to hold the back door in place)
❖ 4⅛″ by 6⅛″ piece of glass (use picture glass, not window glass)
❖ easel stand to display your picture frame

INSTRUCTIONS

Note: When cutting the mat board, place the ruler so it protects the area you plan to keep. That way if the knife strays a bit as you are cutting, it will stray into the excess area of the board.

1. Using the pattern provided on page 124, cut one front and three back pieces, saving the center cutout from one back section to use as the back door.

2. Glue the three back pieces together, one on top of the other, matching the edges exactly. Let dry under a stack of books.

3. Trim ¹⁄₁₆″ off the top and one side edge of the back door piece.

4. Cut and press a 10″ by 13″ piece of the cotton fabric.

5. Using a pencil, lightly trace the moon and stars design and the frame corner points onto the pressed fabric.

6. Paint the design as desired and let dry. Ink in the moon's eye and mouth using the permanent marking pens.

7. Cover the frame's front piece with a thin layer of tacky glue and smooth the remnant of batting onto it. Trim the batting to match the edges.

8. Cut the center from the painted fabric, leaving a 1″ turning allowance as shown. (Fig. 1) Clip into the corners.

9. Lay the painted fabric, faceup, on the batting covered front, matching the inner and outer corners.

10. Wrap the turning allowances of the inner edges to the back and glue in place.

11. Trim the outer edge turning allowances to about 1″ and wrap them around to the back side, smoothing the front as you go. Glue in place.

12. Glue a strip of piping around the inner edge, having the piping show on the front. Clip the piping seam allowance at the corners to make turning the corners easier. (Fig. 2) Repeat for the outer edges.

13. Cover the back in the same manner as the front.

14. Mark the placement of the turn buttonholes on the outside face of the back section. The turn button tab should extend over the back door space about ¼″. (Fig. 3) Use the screw that comes with the turn button to make a hole through the back at each marking. Place a turn button over each hole, matching the holes. Slip a paper brad through the hole and open out the tabs on the opposite side. The turn buttons should be snug, but still able to turn. **Note:** You cannot use the screw to attach the turn button because it is a bit too long and would poke through the front.

15. Cover the outside of the back door piece. Cut a piece of felt that is about ⅛″ smaller than the back door mat board piece and glue it to the inside surface of the back door to cover the turning allowances. (Fig. 4)

16. Glue the front to the back, wrong sides together. Let dry under a stack of books to keep the mat boards from warping.

17. Insert the glass through the back opening, then the picture. Place the back door in the back opening and secure it with the turn buttons.

18. Place the frame on an easel stand to display.

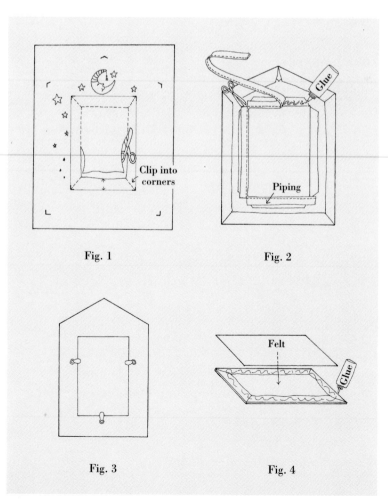

Clip into corners

Fig. 1

Piping

Fig. 2

Felt   Glue

Fig. 3

Fig. 4

Keepsake Box

MATERIALS

❖ 12″ by 12″ remnant of fine cotton batiste
❖ 12″ by 12″ remnant of white flannel
❖ ½ yard of fabric for outside of box
❖ ½ yard of fabric for box lining
❖ embroidery floss DMC colors: 225, 504, 775, 3747, 3823
❖ three 15″ by 20″ sheets of mat or illustration board
❖ tape
❖ 12″ by 12″ sheet of ¼″-thick foam core board
❖ wash-out marking pen or pencil
❖ quilting thread
❖ metal-edge ruler
❖ X-acto® or craft knife
❖ pencil
❖ thin-bodied tacky glue
❖ paper to cover your work surface
❖ 2¼″ yards of ⅛″ cording for trim
❖ 1½ yards of 1″ lace for trim
❖ ½ yard embroidered ribbon for lid paper holders
❖ 1 yard of ¼″ ribbon for lid stops

INSTRUCTIONS

1. Cut the following pieces from the mat board using an X-acto knife and metal-edge ruler.
   A. Lid top center 9″ by 8″ (to be covered with flannel and embroidered fabric)
   B. Lid 11″ by 10″
   C. Lid lining 10¼″ by 9¼″
   D. Outside sides 40″ by 3″ (This will have to be cut in two sections and taped together to get the whole 40″ length; see Fig. 1)
   E. Inside sides 39¼″ by 2¾″ (This will also have to be cut in two sections and taped together, Fig. 2)
   F. Bottom lining 10¼″ by 9¼″ cut from ¼″-thick foam core board
   G. Bottom 11″ by 10″
   Cut the outer fabric and lining fabric to cover the corresponding mat and foam core pieces adding 1″ all around to the above measurements. (Fig. 3) Cut a 10″ by 10″ piece of fabric to make a hinge for the lid.
2. Press the remnant of fine batiste so it is very smooth. Trace the embroidery design onto the center of the batiste using a fine-point wash-out marking pen or pencil.
3. Work the embroidery design according to the pattern on page 125. The colors given are only suggestions; you may like another color combination better. Refer to the Stitch Reference for help with making the stitches.
4. After the embroidered design is complete, wash the piece and iron it dry facedown on a soft cloth.
5. Shadow work depends on an underlining to show off its beauty, so you

will need to cover the top center (A) mat board piece with the white flannel first. Cover one side of the mat board with a thin layer of tacky glue and center it, glued side down, on the wrong side of the flannel. Wrap the turning allowances to the back side of the mat board and glue smoothly in place.

6. Center the embroidered batiste on the flannel-covered mat board. You can either glue the turning allowances to the back side or lace the fabric in place, which leaves more room for fine-tuning the placement of the embroidered piece.

7. To lace, thread a needle with quilting thread that is still on the spool. Unwind about two yards (leaving it attached). Wrap the top and bottom turning allowances to the back side. Adjust and pin the corners to be smooth. Beginning at the right side, run the needle through the turning allowance on the top and then the bottom, making about ½″ stitches. Alternate top and bottom (Fig. 4) until the two edges are pulled in snugly and the front surface is very smooth. You will have to pull more thread off the spool and readjust the lacing stitches as needed. Tie off both ends of the thread.

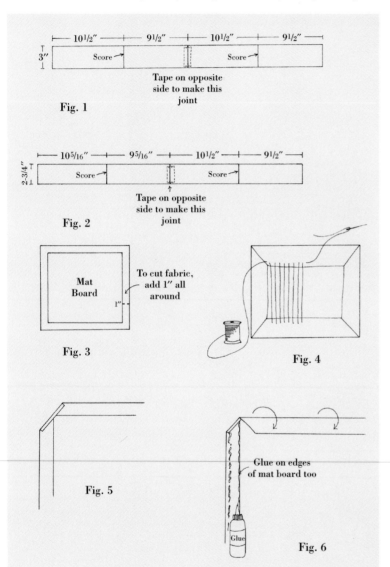

Fig. 1

Fig. 2

Fig. 3

Fig. 4

Fig. 5

Fig. 6

8. Repeat the lacing process for the left and right turning allowances. Stitch the corners closed as well.

9. Cover your work surface with paper to keep the glue mess to a minimum and have a couple of damp rags handy as this job can get messy.

10. Cover one side of the mat board top (B) piece with a thin layer of glue. Lay it glue side down onto the wrong side of its corresponding fabric covering piece. Smooth the fabric completely.

11. Trim the corners diagonally to within ⅛″ of the mat board corner and fold the diagonal-cut corner over the mat board corner and glue down. (Fig. 5)

12. Turn the fabric folding allowances to the back of the mat board and glue down. Be sure to add a bead of glue to the edges of the mat board as well. (Fig. 6)

13. Repeat the above covering procedure to cover the box bottom (G). Cover the box sides in the same manner (the fabric should cover the scored side) but leave one short end unglued to become a gluing tab for assembling the box. (Fig. 7) Cover the foam core bottom lining (F) with lining fabric as well.

14. Center the embroidered panel on the box lid and glue in place. Stack some books on top until the lid dries to get a good bond and keep the mat boards from warping. Let dry overnight.

15. Using the covering technique, cover the lid lining (C) mat board with lining fabric. You can add a layer of batting first if desired.

16. Cut two 8″ lengths of embroidered ribbon and lay each one diagonally across opposite corners. Wrap the cut ends around to the backside and glue in place.

17. Fold the outside sides (D) into a rectangle and glue the fabric tab to the inside. (Fig. 8) Then stitch the joint together carefully to make it more secure.

18. Glue the fabric covered bottom lining (F) into the sides so all edges and surfaces are even at the bottom.

19. Glue the box unit to the covered bottom (G) and stack a few books inside the box to hold it firm while drying. Let dry overnight.

20. Fold the side edges of the fabric hinge piece in ½″ and glue down. (Fig. 9) Then fold in half crosswise, matching the raw edges, and glue the layers together. (Fig. 9)

21. With the folded edges to the sides, lay the hinge fabric on the back side of the lid, having half of the fabric on the lid and half off the lid as shown. (Fig. 10) Glue in place, keeping the glue ¼″ away from the edge of the lid.

22. Lay the box lid facedown on a clean surface. Cut two 12″ lengths of ¼″-wide ribbon and glue one on at each side edge as shown for lid stops. (Fig. 11)

23. Center the covered lid lining (C) on the lid unit, wrong sides together. Glue in place. The hinge fabric and lid stop ribbons will extend from the edges. Place a stack of books on top and let dry overnight.

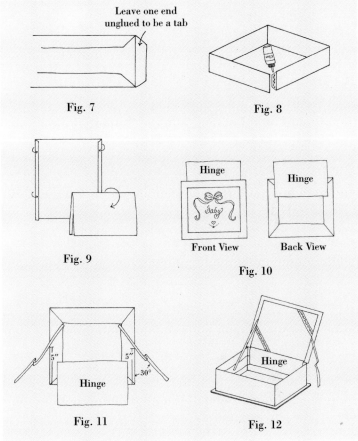

Leave one end unglued to be a tab

Fig. 7

Fig. 8

Fig. 9

Hinge

Front View

Hinge

Back View

Fig. 10

Hinge

Fig. 11

Hinge

Fig. 12

24. Fold the inside side (E) mat board piece to shape, and check the fit inside the box. Trim if necessary and allow a bit of space for the thickness of the fabric you are using. Remember to keep a snug fit.

25. Using the covering technique, cover the inside sides (E) with lining fabric. This time the fabric should cover the unscored side. You do not need to leave a tab at one end on this piece.

26. When the lid unit is completely dry, set the hinge edge on the box as if it were open. Glue the hinge fabric to the inside back of the box. (Fig. 12) Glue the loose ends of the lid stops to the inside of each side. Trim as necessary to fit.

27. Glue the covered inside sides (E) into the box.

28. Glue the lace trim around the top center panel of the lid, tucking the edge of the lace under the panel. Glue the tiny cording around the same edge and also around the joint between the sides and the bottom of the box.

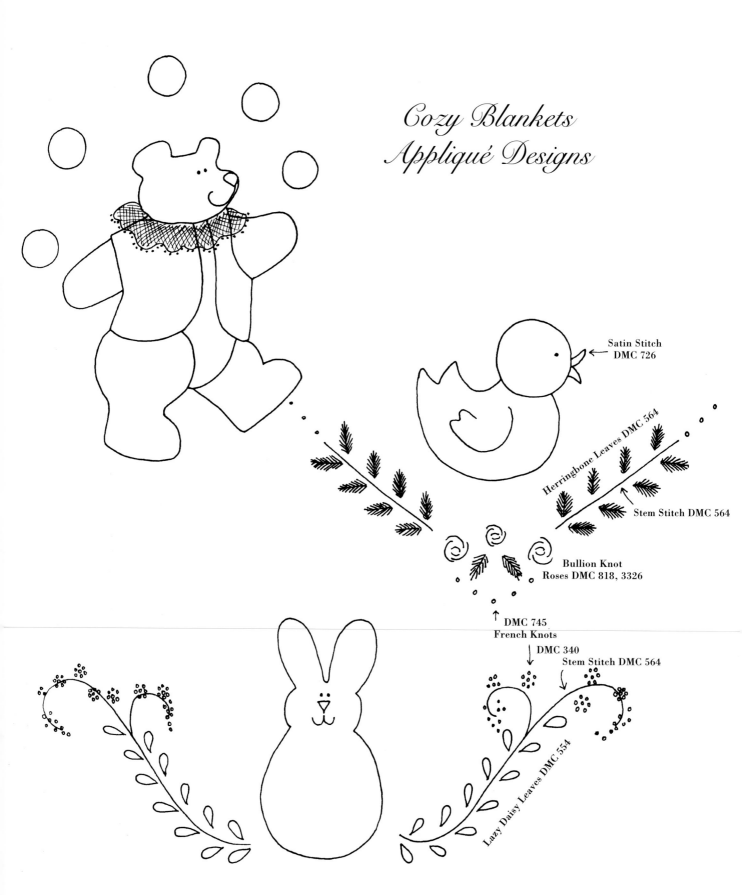

Cozy Blankets
Appliqué Designs

Satin Stitch
DMC 726

Herringbone Leaves DMC 564

Stem Stitch DMC 564

Bullion Knot
Roses DMC 818, 3326

DMC 745
French Knots

DMC 340
Stem Stitch DMC 564

Lazy Daisy Leaves DMC 554

Appliqué Patterns

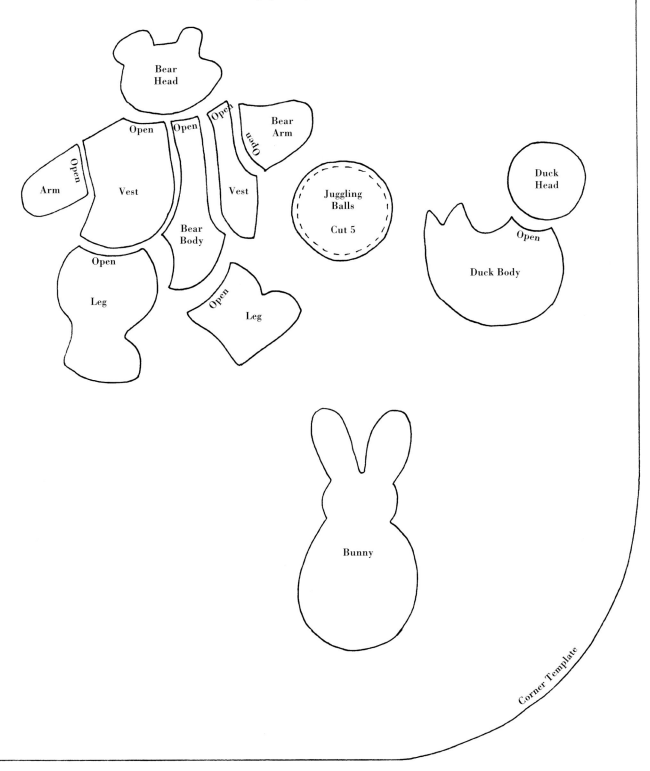

Medium Blue

Med. Blue

Light Blue

Medium Blue

A

Stitching Line

A

Border/Sashing Seam

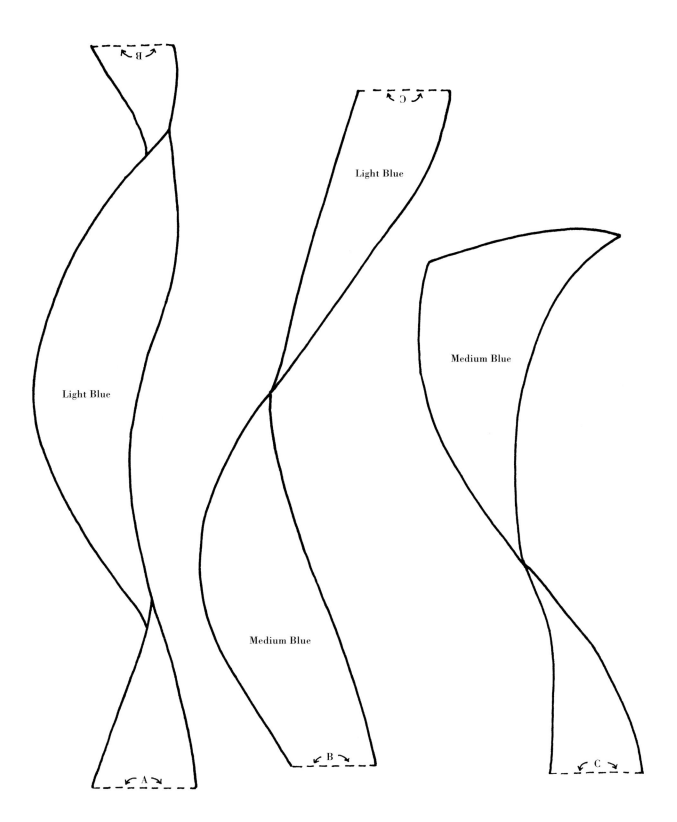

Light Blue

Light Blue

Medium Blue

Medium Blue

Quilt Design for
2" Border

Quilt Design for 6" Border

Quilt Design for 1" Sashing Strips

96

Mobile Lamb Pattern

Mat Cutting Line

Fabric Cutting Line

Lampshade Lambs and Flowers

Baby Cap

Cut 1 on fold
Cut 1 on lining of fold

Place on fold

Center Front

Center Back

Winter Hat

Cut 2
Cut 2 of lining

Center Front

Attach tie here

Center Back

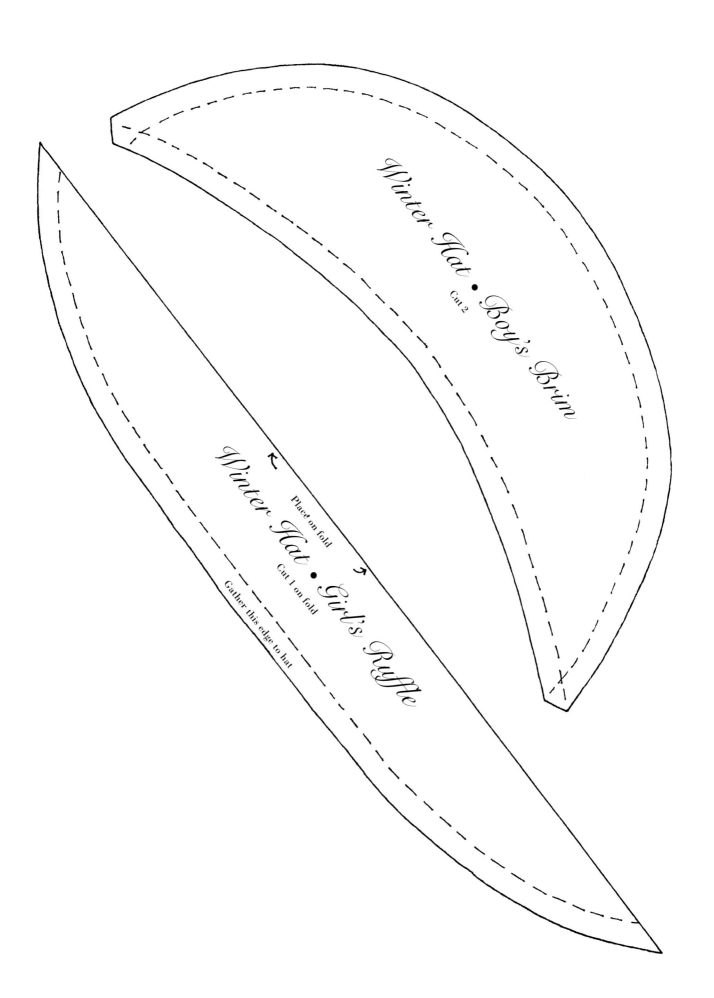

Winter Hat • Boy's Brim
Cut 2

Winter Hat • Girl's Ruffle
Cut 1 on fold

Place on fold

Gather this edge to hat

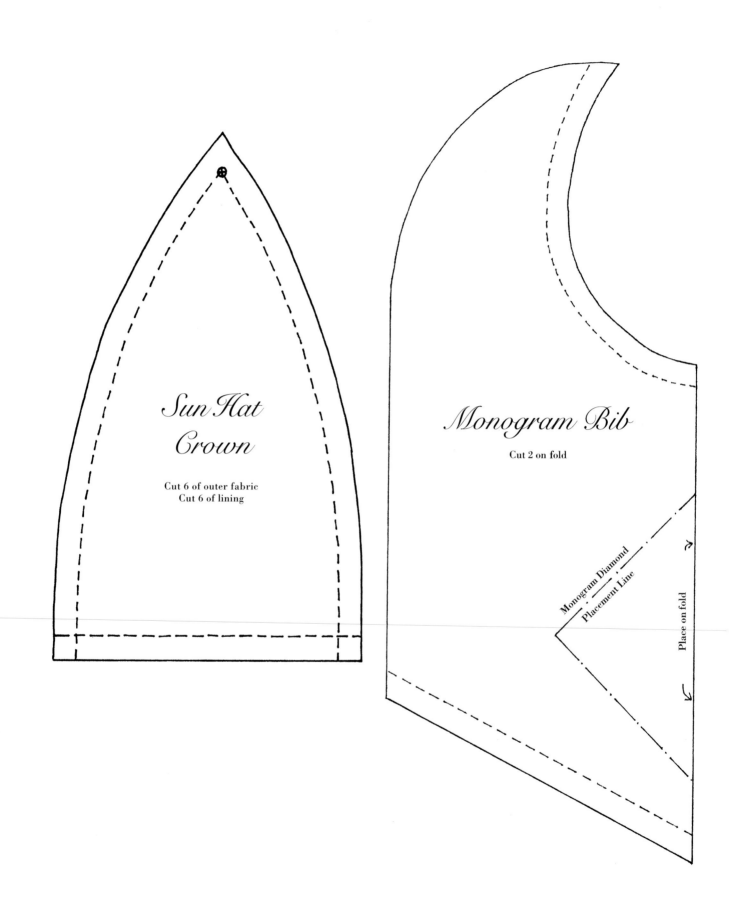

Sun Hat
Crown

Cut 6 of outer fabric
Cut 6 of lining

Monogram Bib

Cut 2 on fold

Monogram Diamond
Placement Line

Place on fold

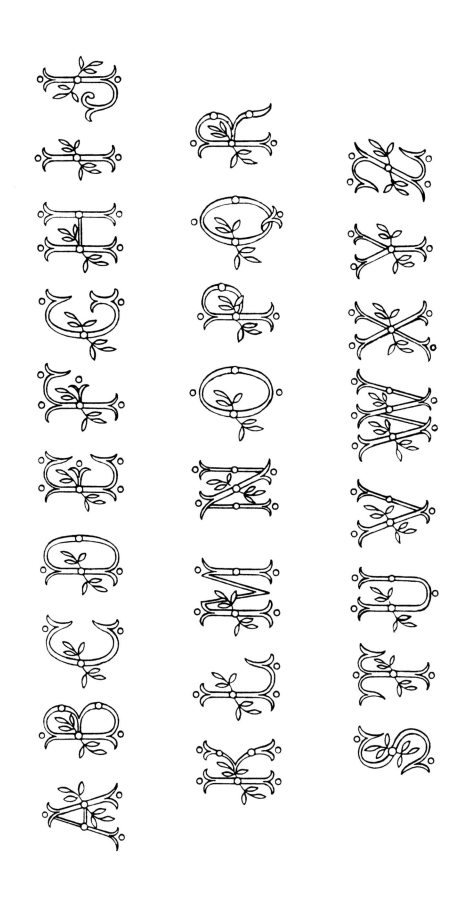

Shadow Work Alphabet

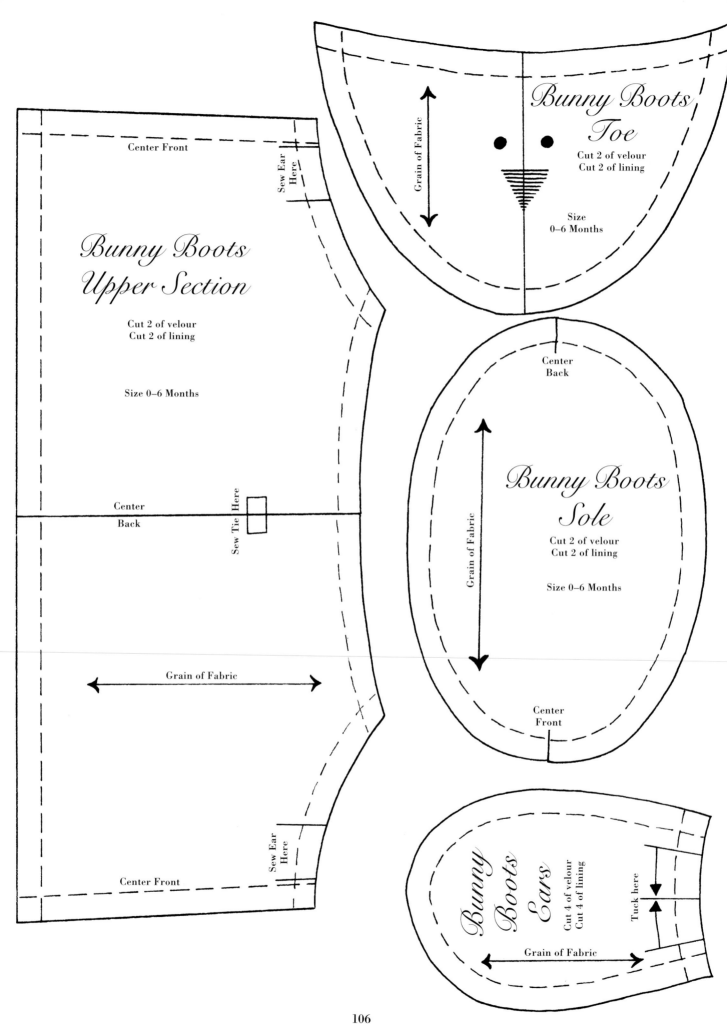

Bunny Boots Toe

Cut 2 of velour
Cut 2 of lining

Grain of Fabric

Size
0–6 Months

Bunny Boots Upper Section

Cut 2 of velour
Cut 2 of lining

Size 0–6 Months

Center Front

Sew Ear Here

Center Back

Sew Tie Here

Grain of Fabric

Sew Ear Here

Center Front

Center Back

Bunny Boots Sole

Cut 2 of velour
Cut 2 of lining

Size 0–6 Months

Grain of Fabric

Center Front

Bunny Boots Ears

Cut 4 of velour
Cut 4 of lining

Tuck here

Grain of Fabric

106

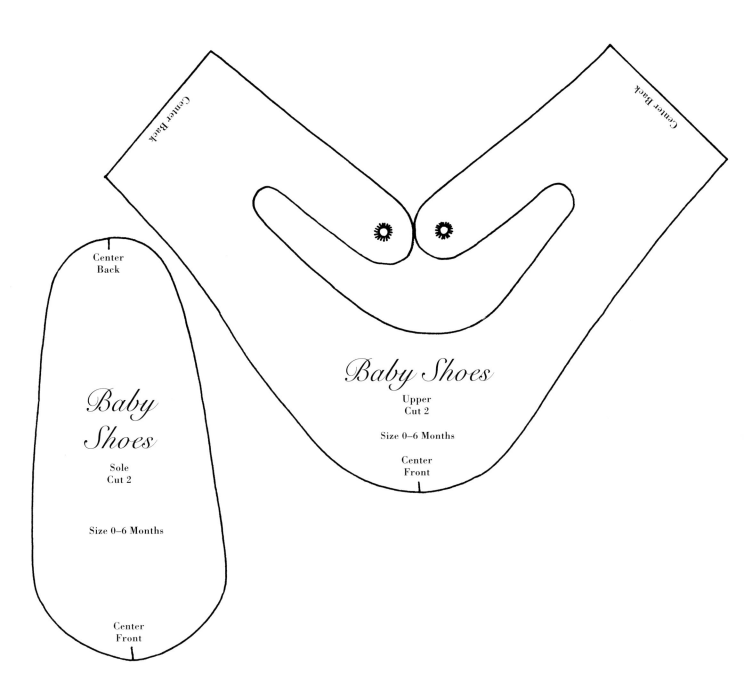

Center
Back

Baby
Shoes

Sole
Cut 2

Size 0–6 Months

Center
Front

Center Back

Center Back

Baby Shoes

Upper
Cut 2

Size 0–6 Months

Center
Front

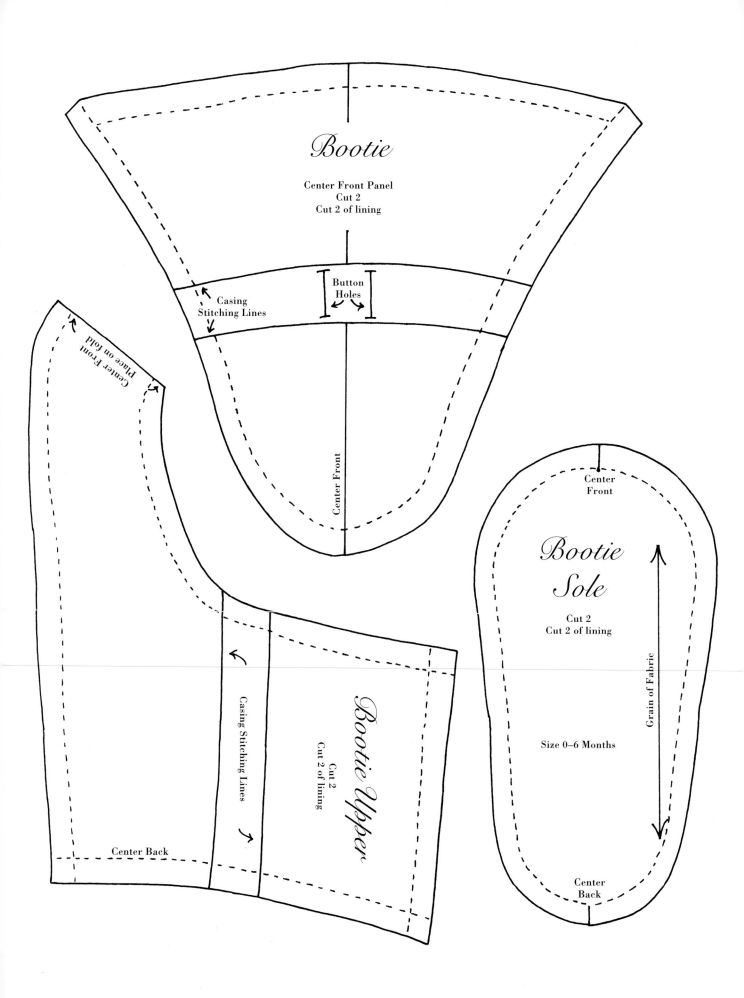

Bootie

Center Front Panel
Cut 2
Cut 2 of lining

Button Holes

Casing Stitching Lines

Center Front Place on fold

Center Front

Casing Stitching Lines

Bootie Upper
Cut 2
Cut 2 of lining

Center Back

Bootie Sole

Center Front

Cut 2
Cut 2 of lining

Size 0–6 Months

Grain of Fabric

Center Back

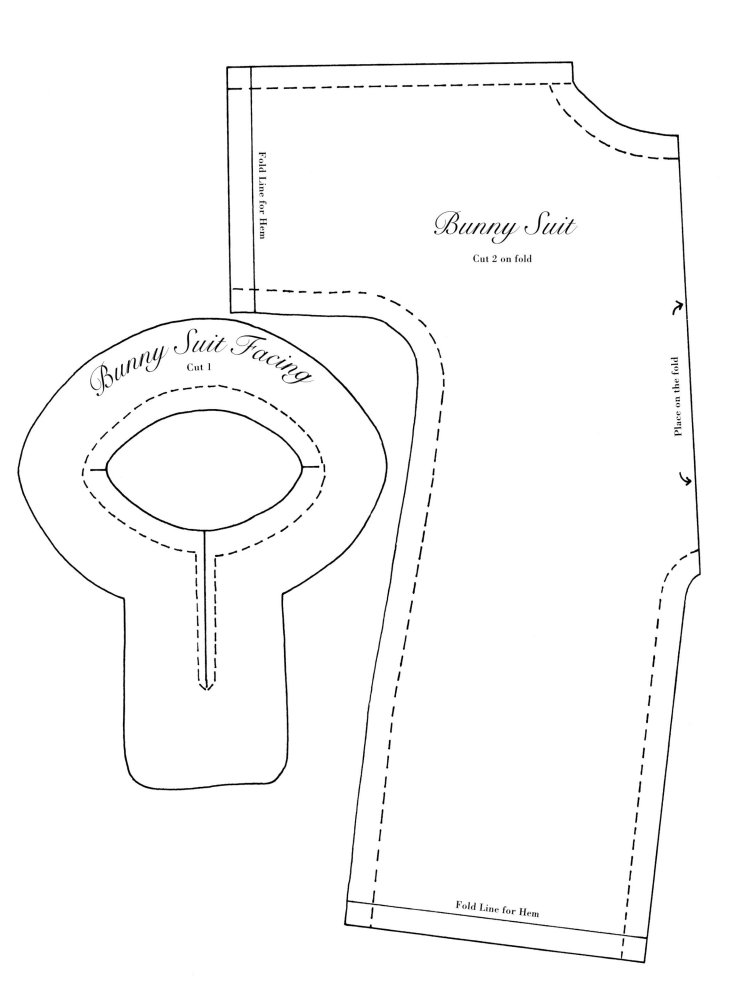

Bunny Suit

Cut 2 on fold

Fold Line for Hem

Place on the fold

Bunny Suit Facing

Cut 1

Fold Line for Hem

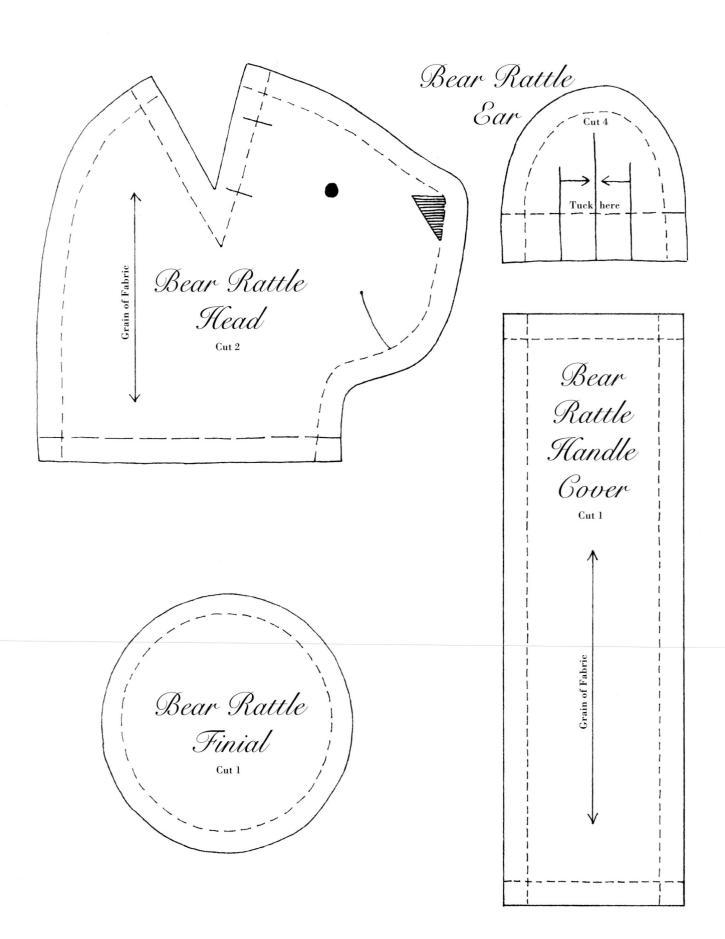

Bear Rattle
Ear

Cut 4

Tuck here

Bear Rattle
Head

Grain of Fabric

Cut 2

Bear
Rattle
Handle
Cover

Cut 1

Grain of Fabric

Bear Rattle
Finial

Cut 1

Hooded Towel • Hood Triangle

Fish Appliqué Patterns

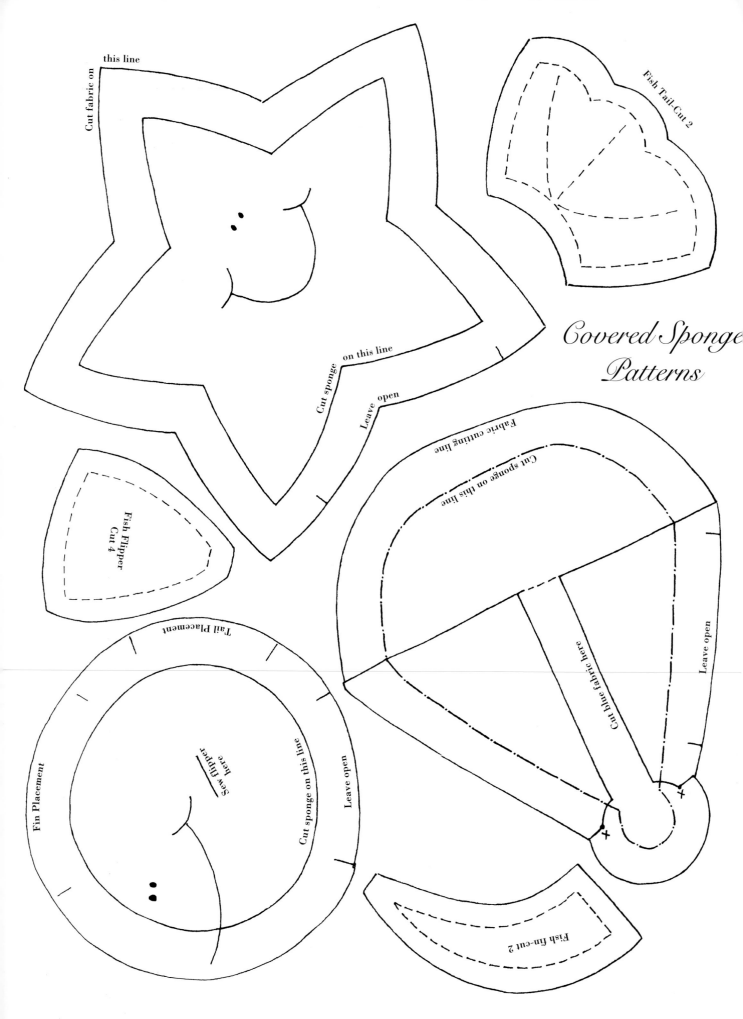

Cut fabric on this line

Fish Tail-Cut 2

Covered Sponge Patterns

Cut sponge on this line

Leave open

Fabric cutting line

Cut sponge on this line

Fish Flipper Cut 4

Cut blue fabric here

Leave open

Tail Placement

Fin Placement

Sew flipper here

Cut sponge on this line

Leave open

Fish fin-cut 2

Appliqué Patterns for Organizer and Bath Mat

Organizer
Top Pocket Fish

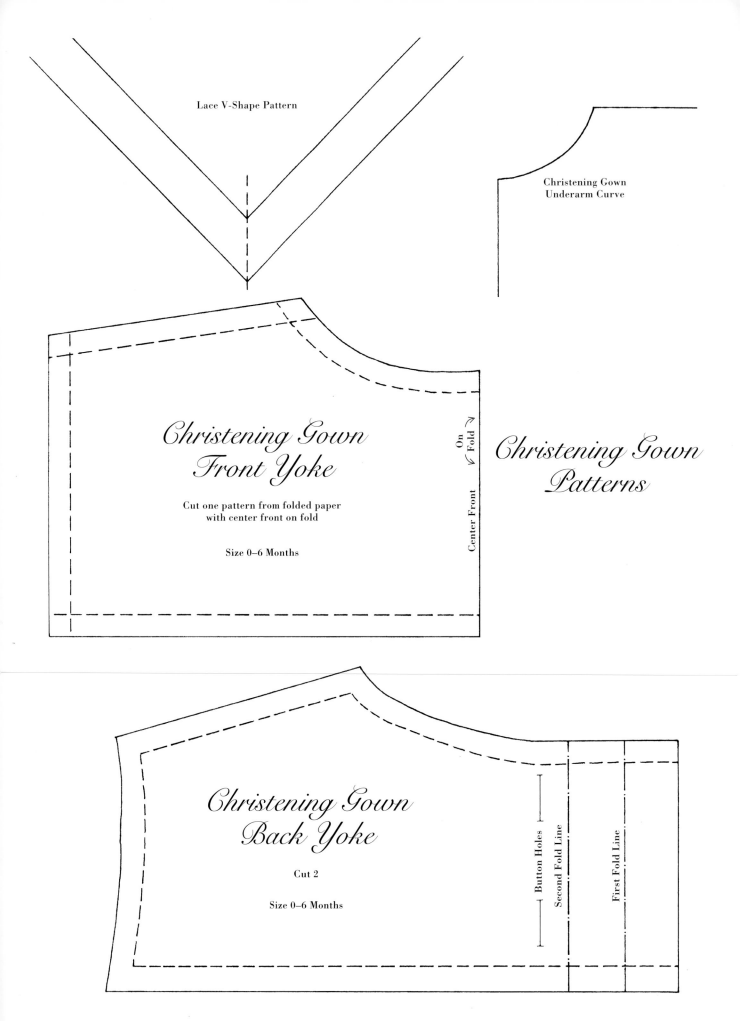

Lace V-Shape Pattern

Christening Gown
Underarm Curve

Christening Gown
Front Yoke

Cut one pattern from folded paper
with center front on fold

Size 0–6 Months

On Fold

Center Front

Christening Gown
Patterns

Christening Gown
Back Yoke

Cut 2

Size 0–6 Months

Button Holes

Second Fold Line

First Fold Line

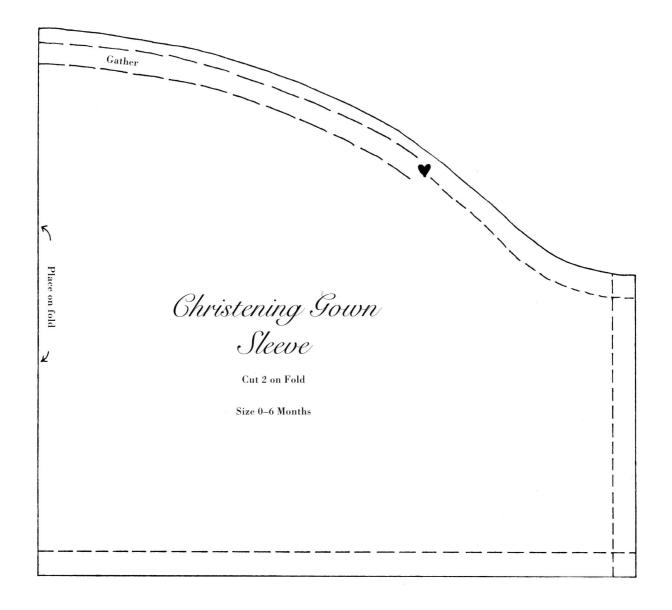

Gather

Place on fold

Christening Gown
Sleeve

Cut 2 on Fold

Size 0–6 Months

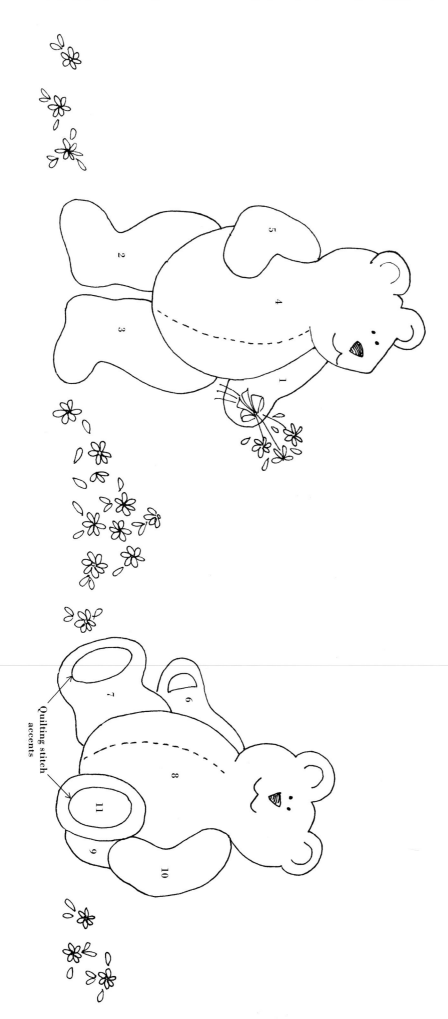

Carriage Blanket Appliqué Design

Quilting stitch
accents

Padded Satin Stitch

See colors on page 79.

abcdefghijklmnopqrstuvwxyz
ABCDEFGHIJKLMNOPQ
RSTUVWXYZ
1234567890

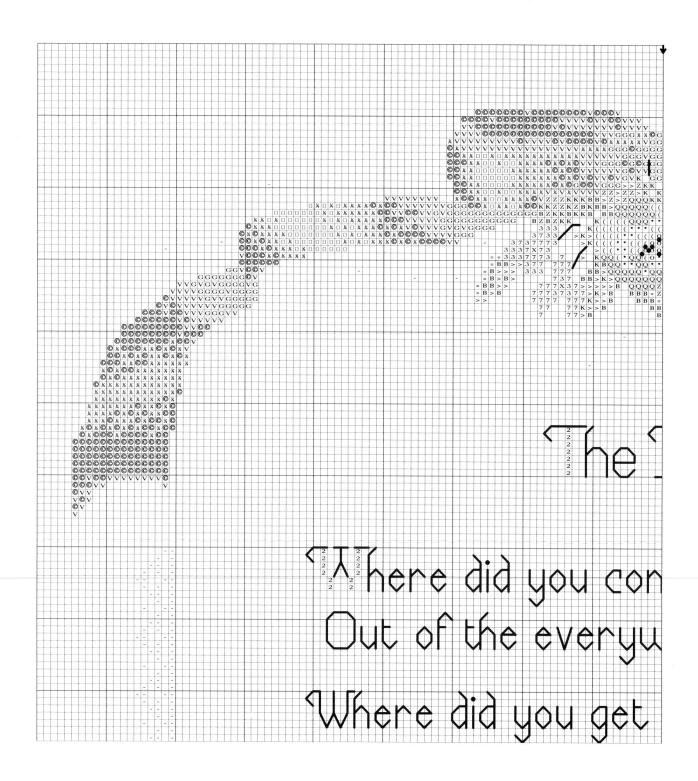

here did you con

Out of the everyu

Where did you get

Baby

ne from, baby dear?

uhere, into the here.

your eyes so blue?

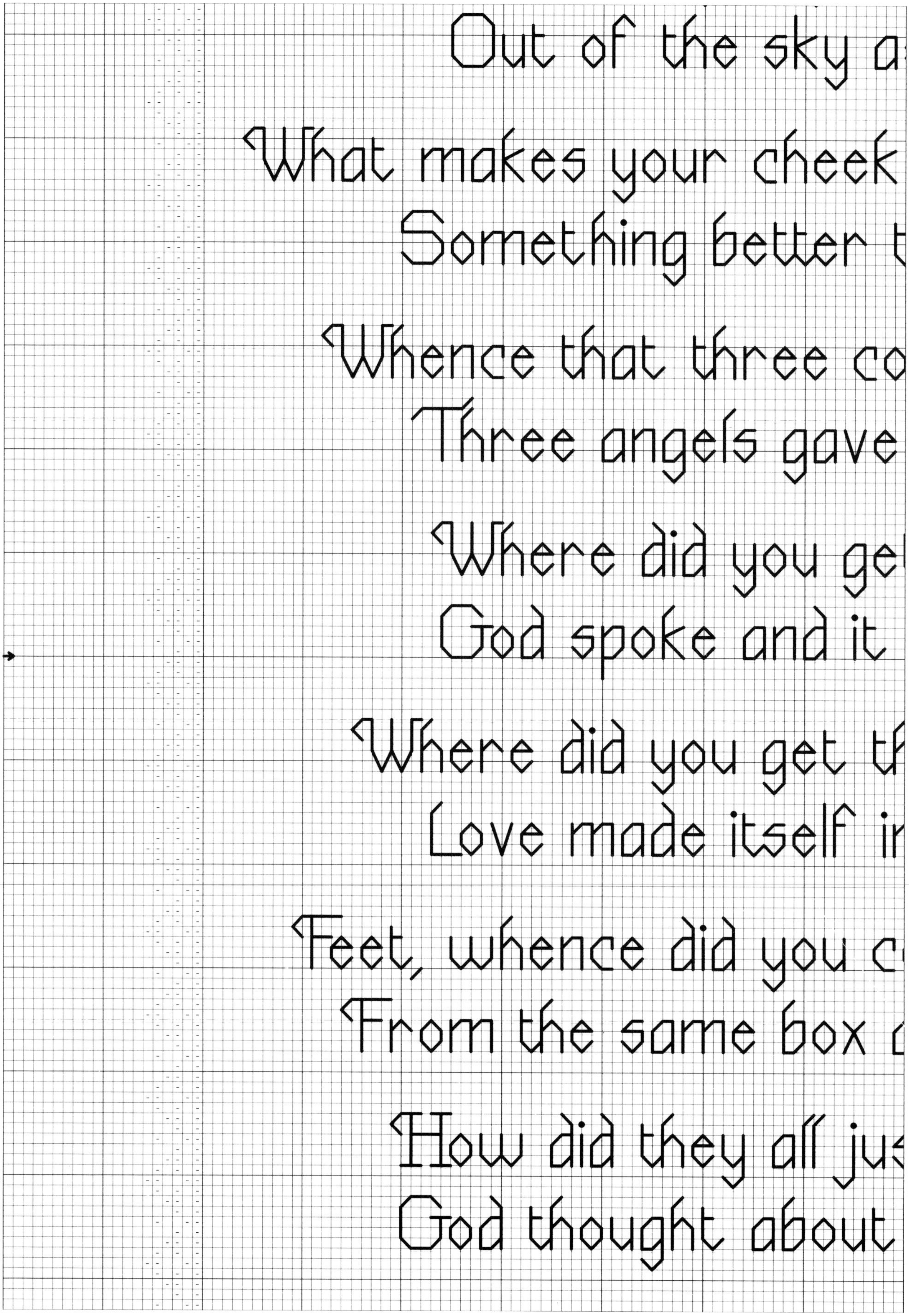

Out of the sky a

What makes your cheek

Something better t

Whence that three co

Three angels gave

Where did you ge

God spoke and it

Where did you get tf

Love made itself in

Feet, whence did you c

From the same box o

How did they all jus

God thought about

s I came through.

like a warm white rose?

han anyone knows

rnered smile of bliss!

me at once a kiss.

t that pearly ear?

came out to hear.

hose arms and hands?

to hooks and bands.

ome, you darling things?

as the cherubs' wings.

st come to be you?

me and so I grew.

me to us you dear?

you and so I am here.

MacDonald

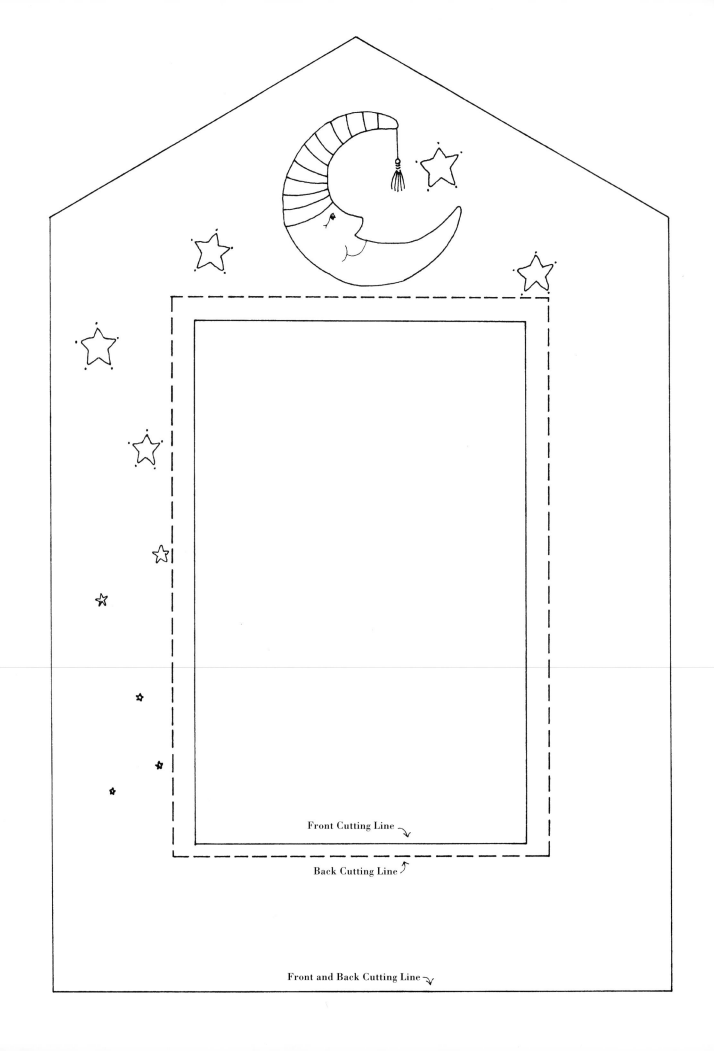

Front Cutting Line

Back Cutting Line

Front and Back Cutting Line

Keepsake Box Shadow Work Pattern

DMC 225   Heart, large center flower, and underside of bird
DMC 504   Stems and leaves
DMC 775   Top of birds, wings, and eyes
DMC 3747 Lettering, bow, smaller flowers, and dots next to heart
DMC 3823 Small dots

Stitch Reference

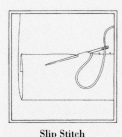

Slip Stitch

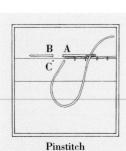

Running Stitch

Pinstitch

Fig. 1

Pinstitch

Fig. 2

Slip Stitch

Use a #8 or #10 crewel or sharp needle for the slip stitch. Knot the end of the thread. Bring the needle up through the hem fold of the fabric, catch two or three threads of the base fabric and run the needle back into the hem fold and out again ¼″ away.

Running Stitch

The running stitch is the simplest of all sewing stitches and is also the most versatile. Use this stitch for basting (a longer stitch length), quilting (a shorter stitch length), or in embroidery or cross-stitch for decoration. It is a simple in-and-out motion of the needle in the fabric, but it does take a bit of practice to keep all the stitches the same length. (See diagram)

Pinstitch

Use a #26 tapestry needle for the pin stitch. You will need to put the needle through the same hole a couple of times and the blunt point of the tapestry needle will help.

Take a small back stitch to secure the thread. Insert the needle at point A and out at point B. (Fig. 1) Then stitch from point A to point C. (Fig. 2) These two movements make one stitch unit. Now point B becomes point A for the next stitch. Continue stitching A to B and A to C. Keep the stitches pulled firmly as you work. To end the thread, push the needle to the back and ease it through several of the diagonal stitches.

Split Stitch

The split stitch is best worked with the fabric stretched in an embroidery hoop, using the stab stitch method. Take a tiny back stitch at the beginning of the pattern, ending with the needle at the back. Push the needle up through the fabric and the previous stitch, splitting the thread of that stitch about one third of the length from the end. Push the needle back down through the fabric about ⅛″ away and repeat the process.

Stem Stitch

Use one strand of embroidery floss and a #10 crewel needle for the stem stitch. A stem stitch is a very simple stitch to work. The needle will point in the opposite direction of the direction you are stitching. Even though the stitches will look slanted, resist the temptation to insert the needle at a slant to your marked line. Always keep the thread above the needle as it comes out of the fabric. (See diagram)

Lazy Daisy Stitch

For the lazy daisy stitch, bring the needle up at A. Reinsert the needle at A and out at B, having the thread wrap under the needle. (Fig. 1) Pull the needle and thread through, but not tightly. Push the needle back down at B, anchoring the loop at that point. (Fig. 2)

Split Stitch

Stem Stitch

Lazy Daisy Stitch

Fig. 1

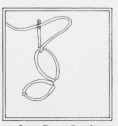

Lazy Daisy Stitch

Fig. 2

Padded Satin Stitch

Fig. 1

Padded Satin Stitch

Fig. 2

Padded Satin Stitch

Fig. 3

Padded Satin Stitch

Fig. 4

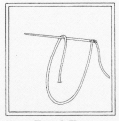

French Knot

Fig. 1

Padded Satin Stitch

For the padded satin stitch, first outline the design to be stitched using a tiny split stitch. This will make a wall to build the rest of the stitches in and around. (Fig. 1) To create the first layer of padding, make some stitches side by side in one direction, keeping the stitches in from the edges a bit. (Fig. 2) Make another layer of padding stitches going crosswise to the first layer and a little closer to the edges. (Fig. 3) As you do the first two layers of padding, practice keeping the stitches even and close together, so when you get to the top layer you have the feel of making nice, even stitches to get a smooth finish. For the final layer, the needle should enter the fabric on the outside of and just under the split stitch wall, and exit the same way on the opposite side, one thread width away from the previous stitch. (Fig. 4)

French Knot

The French knot stitch is widely used in many types of embroidery. Wrap the thread around the needle only once for each knot. This will keep the knot tight and well-shaped. If you wrap the thread around the needle more than once, the knot can get uneven and lopsided. If you need a larger knot, simply use more strands of floss.

To make the French knot, bring the needle up through the fabric at the place you want the knot. Hold the needle horizontally and wrap the thread over the needle. (Fig. 1) Now insert the needle into the fabric about two fabric threads away from the original point. Push the needle in about halfway and pull the thread so the loop is snug around the needle and rests on the fabric surface. (Fig. 2) Keep tension on the thread and pull the needle through to finish the knot.

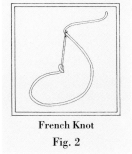

French Knot

Fig. 2

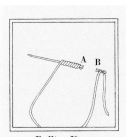

Bullion Knot

Fig. 1

Bullion Knot

The bullion knot stitch is a wonderful stitch to learn. You can use it in so many ways in your embroidery—make leaves, rosebuds, roses, three, four, and five petal flowers, and bumblebees. (Fig. 1) Use a #10 crewel needle and one strand of floss. Bring the needle up at point A. Insert the needle at B and back out at A, push the needle through up to the eye (Fig. 2), and wrap the thread around the needle the desired number of times. Keep the wraps firm and smooth, but not tight. Grasp the wraps on the needle with your index finger and thumb, and pull the needle through with your other hand. As you near the end of the thread, the wraps will pull back around to cover the A to B stitch length. (Fig. 3) You can shape the curve

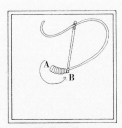

Bullion Knot

Fig. 2

Bullion Knot

Fig. 3

of the stitch by placing your thumb firmly on top of the stitches and pulling the thread around in the direction you want the knot to curve. To complete the stitch, insert the needle into the fabric one or two fabric threads away from point B.

If you want the finished knot to be straight, the length of the wraps should equal the length of the stitch from A to B. If you want a curved knot, the length of the wraps on the needle should be a bit longer than the length of the stitch from A to B. If you want to make loops, as for the petal flowers, the length from A to B should be very tiny (two or three fabric threads) and the wraps as desired to make the size of petal you want.

Herringbone Leaf Stitch

For the herringbone leaf stitch, use a #10 crewel needle and one strand of floss. Bring the needle to the front of the fabric at the tip of the leaf. Taking a small stitch, insert the needle at the vein of the leaf and out again just to the right of the original thread on the leaf outline. (Fig. 1) Take the second stitch in at the vein, one fabric thread below the first stitch, and out at the left side of the first stitch on the leaf outline. (Fig. 2) Repeat the process, entering on the leaf vein and alternating left and right exit points (Fig. 3) to fill in the leaf shape. (Fig. 4) The vein does not have to be in the center of the leaf.

Shadow Work

Shadow work is a beautiful and easy stitching technique to learn. It is a double back stitch in which the thread is carried from side to side to create a shadow of the color showing through the delicate fabric on which it is worked. Work this embroidery with the fabric stretched in an embroidery hoop. Use a #26 tapestry needle and one strand of floss. The fabric you are working on should be sheer; cotton Swiss batiste or organdy produces very nice results.

To begin, knot the end of the thread and insert the needle through the top of the fabric so the knot is on the surface (to be cut away later) and the thread on the back will be in the path of the design, so the crisscrossing thread of the actual shadow stitching will anchor the beginning thread in place. Bring the needle up at A and down at B. (Fig. 1) Then up at C and down at B (Fig. 2) Then up at D and down at A, then up at E and down at C, and so on. When making the stitches, the down stitch always goes into the hole of the previous stitch on the side you are working. Continue making these backstitches, alternating sides. The number of stitches on each side of the design being stitched must be the same. When working on curves, the stitches on the outside curve will have to be longer than the stitches on the inside curve. On very tight curves it is sometimes necessary to make an inside curve stitch two times to keep the alternating rows of stitches even with each other. To end the thread, weave it through the crisscrossed stitches on the back.

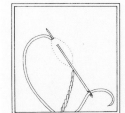

Fig. 1

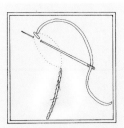

Fig. 2

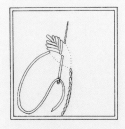

Fig. 3

Fig. 4

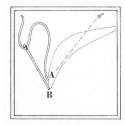

Fig. 1

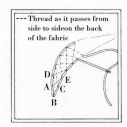

--- Thread as it passes from side to side on the back of the fabric

Fig. 2

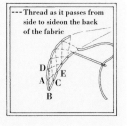

--- Thread as it passes from side to side on the back of the fabric

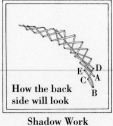

How the back side will look

Shadow Work